Education in a Competitive and Globalizing World

Science and Technology Education

Perspectives, Opportunities and Challenges

EDUCATION IN A COMPETITIVE AND GLOBALIZING WORLD

Additional books in this series can be found on Nova's website under the Series tab.

Additional e-books in this series can be found on Nova's website under the eBooks tab.

EDUCATION IN A COMPETITIVE AND GLOBALIZING WORLD

SCIENCE AND TECHNOLOGY EDUCATION

PERSPECTIVES, OPPORTUNITIES AND CHALLENGES

STEFFEN PABST
EDITOR

Copyright © 2018 by Nova Science Publishers, Inc.

All rights reserved. No part of this book may be reproduced, stored in a retrieval system or transmitted in any form or by any means: electronic, electrostatic, magnetic, tape, mechanical photocopying, recording or otherwise without the written permission of the Publisher.

We have partnered with Copyright Clearance Center to make it easy for you to obtain permissions to reuse content from this publication. Simply navigate to this publication's page on Nova's website and locate the "Get Permission" button below the title description. This button is linked directly to the title's permission page on copyright.com. Alternatively, you can visit copyright.com and search by title, ISBN, or ISSN.

For further questions about using the service on copyright.com, please contact:
Copyright Clearance Center
Phone: +1-(978) 750-8400   Fax: +1-(978) 750-4470   E-mail: info@copyright.com.

NOTICE TO THE READER

The Publisher has taken reasonable care in the preparation of this book, but makes no expressed or implied warranty of any kind and assumes no responsibility for any errors or omissions. No liability is assumed for incidental or consequential damages in connection with or arising out of information contained in this book. The Publisher shall not be liable for any special, consequential, or exemplary damages resulting, in whole or in part, from the readers' use of, or reliance upon, this material. Any parts of this book based on government reports are so indicated and copyright is claimed for those parts to the extent applicable to compilations of such works.

Independent verification should be sought for any data, advice or recommendations contained in this book. In addition, no responsibility is assumed by the publisher for any injury and/or damage to persons or property arising from any methods, products, instructions, ideas or otherwise contained in this publication.

This publication is designed to provide accurate and authoritative information with regard to the subject matter covered herein. It is sold with the clear understanding that the Publisher is not engaged in rendering legal or any other professional services. If legal or any other expert assistance is required, the services of a competent person should be sought. FROM A DECLARATION OF PARTICIPANTS JOINTLY ADOPTED BY A COMMITTEE OF THE AMERICAN BAR ASSOCIATION AND A COMMITTEE OF PUBLISHERS.

Additional color graphics may be available in the e-book version of this book.

Library of Congress Cataloging-in-Publication Data

ISBN: 978-1-53613-717-0

Published by Nova Science Publishers, Inc. † New York

CONTENTS

Preface   **vii**

Chapter 1   Models of Scientific Identity   **1**
                        Saima Salehjee and Mike Watts

Chapter 2   Strategy versus Reality in Technology Education
                        at Basic Schools in Slovakia   **63**
                        Alena Hašková and Silvia Manduľáková

Chapter 3   Male and Female Technological Talents
                        and Their Motivated Behavioral Choices
                        during the Last Twenty Years   **99**
                        Ossi Autio

Chapter 4   Learning Science in the SDGs Era:
                        Opportunities for Building Youth Competency   **125**
                        Seyoung Hwang

Index   **147**

PREFACE

In this book, the authors examine a series of key science identity-based research models with the goal of discussing the interplay between individual agency and social interaction through the lens of transformative learning. Current identity-based models are critiqued based on the importance given to either social structures and/or agency separately. Following this, a synthesis report on the development strategies of technology education carried out at basic schools in Slovakia (lower secondary education – ISCED 2) is presented. Additionally, the authors discuss the results of a survey done with the goal of finding out the reality of technology teaching at these schools. As the research results show, despite the good intentions of the different strategies, programs and reforms, the technology education at basic schools is on the decline. The next chapter discusses gender-based segregation and falling recruitment for scientific and technological studies in Nordic countries. This study traced and interviewed students who achieved the best results in the measurement of technological competence twenty years ago in order to examine their progress. In the final study, the book proposes a new vision for science education in the era of sustainable development. The authors discuss how sustainable development goals (SDGs) identify new roles for science and technology to address global and local challenges such as climate change, energy innovation, and biodiversity. These areas of sustainability reveal new horizons for science education by enabling us to approach science learning as a more community-based practice and collaborative way of thinking, beyond classroom-based learning.

Chapter 1 - This chapter examines a series of key science identity-based research models. The authors' purpose is to discuss the interplay of individual agency and social interaction through the lens of transformative learning. The authors critique those current identity-based models based on the importance given to either social structures and/or agency separately. The authors also review contemporary research on transformational learning and identity change, illustrating transformation or movement of learners towards, or away from, the study of science. The chapter is a contribution to the debates concerning the considerable impact of identity construction on learning, and the construction of 'science-identity' in particular. With this in mind, the authors examine the central issues in the light of the teaching and learning of science in schools and universities, as well as in the population at large. Our core argument is that an understanding and analysis of these models and theories leads to the design of a conjugated theoretical model of 'science identity' (Sci-ID) consisting of seven main interconnected and interlinked 'slices'. These seven slices represent the (i) global forces (GF: such as gender, ethnicity, race and class) experienced by learners, (ii) social agencies and agents (SA: such as schools, other institutes, parents and teachers) personifying global forces, (iii) transformational learning (TL) experiences (accidental and/or planned events, triggers and interventions) shaping (iv) personal preferences, (v) meaning, and (vi) individual internal agency (IIA) directed by the inner most (vii) central core impacting upon individuals' subject and career choices. Our concluding summary encompasses: (a) identities that are fluid and stable – with the journey towards stability depends on factors such as, for example, age, experiences, relationships, events, triggers, etc. (b) identities that are not entirely fluid, where there are forms of stability, a kind of internal force or agency that empowers people in accepting or declining the influences from the external forces; and (c) the ways in which one's identity depends on the strength of certain GF, SA, TL experiences (events, triggers, interventions) and the strength of one's IIA that goes with it or against it.

Preface

Chapter 2 - Technology has always constituted an important facet of culture. The progress of technology has influenced - even determined – the development of every type of society. This is why technology education represents, or at least should represent, an essential component of general education. This chapter presents on the one hand a synthesis report on the development strategies of technology education carried out at basic schools in Slovakia (lower secondary education – ISCED 2) and on the other hand the results of survey research aimed at revealing the practical reality of technology teaching at these schools (the approaches of students, teachers and school leaders to technology education; the status of subjects within technology education and their curricula; the creation of appropriate conditions for teaching technology education etc.). The education policy of the European Union calls for the support of school development and the modernization and improvement in quality of education. In accordance with the policy of the EU, in their *Reports on the State of the Education System and Systematic Steps for its Development* successive Slovak governments have announced a national education policy and within that significant attention has also been paid to technology education at all levels of education. In the synthesis report, government announcements aimed at the support of technology education and steps adopted by government are analyzed, and the relevant benefits and costs are evaluated. Ultimately, despite some differences in the government announcements, each of them declares support for further development of vocational education and increasing students' interest in it (in accordance with labor market needs). To discover the reality, i.e., to find out how education policy statements related to technology education and related legislation are reflected in practice, and to find out their impact on teaching practice at the lower level of secondary education, survey research was carried out. The research was based on semi-structured personal interviews with technology teachers working at basic schools, via a research sample in which all regions of Slovakia were represented. As the research results show, despite the proclaimed good intentions of the different strategies, programs and reforms, the reality is different – the most worrying finding is that the status of the subject of technology (by means of which technology education at basic schools is carried out) is on the decline. So the questions are: What are the reasons for this state of affairs? What should be done about it? What are the challenges for schools/decision makers resulting from this state of affairs?

Chapter 3 - Gender-based segregation and falling recruitment for scientific and technological studies are common phenomena in all Nordic countries. Furthermore, a great deal of research has been done and a wide variety of programs has been developed to increase female participation in careers such as engineering and physical science. This chapter is connected with an earlier research that assessed technological competence among adolescents. Later on, this study traced and interviewed the students, who achieved the best results in the measurement of technological competence twenty years ago. The aim of this present study was to examine how these three best males and females have progressed in twenty years. Are they working in technology as well or did they end up in other professions? Although the authors must be cautious about the conclusions because of the limited number of research subjects, the study shows that it is possible to predict students' potential for ending in a technological career. However, the process in making motivated behavioral choices in the area of technology seems to be much more complicated for technologically talented females than for males.

Chapter 4 - In this study, the authors propose a new vision for science education in the era of sustainable development goals. In the first section of the chapter, the authors discuss how the sustainable development goals (SDGs) identify new roles for science and technology to address global and local challenges such as climate change, energy innovation, and biodiversity. These areas of sustainability reveal new visions for science education by enabling us to approach science learning as a more community-based practice and collaborative way of thinking, beyond classroom-based learning. Based on this idea, the chapter presents 'youth sustainability competency' as an educational concept for identifying and discussing methods of promoting young people's engagement with SDGs issues. The authors also illustrate an example of such learning by focusing on a youth internship program in a community garden in New York City and a national youth center in South Korea. The focus of the analysis was to identify the elements of youth sustainable competency and to discuss how youth engagement can be facilitated in ways which build youth competency through science and technology education while also addressing SDGs.

In: Science and Technology Education
Editor: Steffen Pabst

ISBN: 978-1-53613-717-0
© 2018 Nova Science Publishers, Inc.

Chapter 1

MODELS OF SCIENTIFIC IDENTITY

Saima Salehjee[1,] and Mike Watts[2]*
[1]School of Education, University of Strathclyde,
Glasgow, Scotland, UK
[2]Department of Education, Brunel Univeristy London,
London, England, UK.

ABSTRACT

This chapter examines a series of key science identity-based research models. Our purpose is to discuss the interplay of individual agency and social interaction through the lens of transformative learning. We critique those current identity-based models based on the importance given to either social structures and/or agency separately. We also review contemporary research on transformational learning and identity change, illustrating transformation or movement of learners towards, or away from, the study of science. The chapter is a contribution to the debates concerning the considerable impact of identity construction on learning, and the construction of 'science-identity' in particular. With this in mind, we examine the central issues in the light of the teaching and learning of science in schools and universities, as well as in the population at large.

---

[*] Corresponding Author Email: saima.salehjee@strath.ac.uk.

Our core argument is that an understanding and analysis of these models and theories leads to the design of a conjugated theoretical model of 'science identity' (Sci-ID) consisting of seven main interconnected and interlinked 'slices'. These seven slices represent the (i) global forces (GF: such as gender, ethnicity, race and class) experienced by learners, (ii) social agencies and agents (SA: such as schools, other institutes, parents and teachers) personifying global forces, (iii) transformational learning (TL) experiences (accidental and/or planned events, triggers and interventions) shaping (iv) personal preferences, (v) meaning, and (vi) individual internal agency (IIA) directed by the inner most (vii) central core impacting upon individuals' subject and career choices.

Our concluding summary encompasses: (a) identities that are fluid and stable – with the journey towards stability depends on factors such as, for example, age, experiences, relationships, events, triggers, etc. (b) identities that are not entirely fluid, where there are forms of stability, a kind of internal force or agency that empowers people in accepting or declining the influences from the external forces; and (c) the ways in which one's identity depends on the strength of certain GF, SA, TL experiences (events, triggers, interventions) and the strength of one's IIA that goes with it or against it.

Keywords: identity, agency, structure, science identity, stable identity, fluid identity

INTRODUCTION

This chapter is an attempt to understand why some students will continue with their studies of science while others do not. It builds on a considerable body of educational research on identity: in this case, being – or not being – a 'science person'. As Darragh (2016) points out, identity is a lens that is adjustable; one that can zoom in (Lerman, 2001) to the level of interactions between individuals or zoom out to look at the wider socio-political context (Stinson & Bullock, 2012). This highlights a significant division in the literature between 'zoomed out' social identity, how one believes others perceive you, and a 'zoom in' on personal identity, how one sees oneself. There are numerous factors that contribute to social forms of identity, which at first glance may seem to exist outside of formal (school- and university-based) science education – such as gender, race, religion, social class and socioeconomic status. It is clear from studies in this area (for example, Archer et al., 2016) that students in some social groups (for instance, middle class, Asian males) have easier experiences identifying as a science person than do others (by contrast, white, working class girls). In our review, however, we focus on and look rather harder at subjective, individual level of identity than the broadly social, and work to understand learners' personal relationships with science. No doubt their 'personal identity' interacts significantly with their 'social identity' – not least through praise or disapproval by peers, parents, teachers, tutors. In this chapter, though, we have chosen to foreground the personal over the social. As Nunes et al. (2017) point out, studies using socio-cultural perspective to investigate the teaching and learning of science education for low socio-economic status (SES) pupils dominate the research. In this chapter, while we begin with a broad social sweep, we center very rapidly on to the individual formation of identity and its relation to a young person's sense of being 'sciencey'.

A distinct trend in studies of identity can be traced to Carol Dweck's work on 'self-theories' and 'mindset' (1999, 2008) so that young people are seen to have either an 'entity' (fixed) view of their abilities, or an 'incremental' (growth) view. Our own research (Salehjee & Watts, 2015; Salehjee, 2017) introduces a nuanced version of this. We also posit two kinds of students: the first type sees their 'science disposition' as stable – fixed either positively for or adamantly against science. These are students who, on the one hand, see themselves as determinedly (pro-) science or, on the other hand, avowedly non-sciencey. The second type of students are fluid in regards to science – their dispositions are much more malleable: they can go with it, side against it or stay openly neutral, depending on circumstances, contexts and experiences. In this chapter we review literature that has directed us towards this set of outcomes and, in the final sections, discuss a particular composite model of science identity (the Sci-ID model) that owes a good deal to Jack Mezirow's (2000) and Knud Illeris (2014) theories of transformational learning.

REVIEWS OF THE NATURE OF IDENTITY

Identity-based research has a long tradition in education, and is mirrored in science education (Lee, 2012). At heart, the debate is neatly captured in the reflective paper by Albright et al. (2008): the extent to which the construction of identity is an expression of 'internal' individual agency or of 'external' cultural and social forces. They make the obvious, but relevant point that identity is conceptualized and bounded by the theoretical frameworks used, with identity being 'a slippery eel to grasp when it comes to informing educational practice' (p. 146). The classical division here is whether a young person's early 'dispositions' or 'identity' are driven primarily by personal identity or social identity, that is by 'individual internal agency', or the greater 'global forces' of social structures. As Block (2013, p.126) has stated, the theoretical rigidity between structure and agency is a 'tension often mentioned but seldom explored in depth'. The third way, of course, is that such polarities are iniquitous, both sets of factors are vitally important. This third way is nicely captured by Giddens (1979) when he stated that 'structure enters simultaneously into the constitution of the agent and social practices, and 'exists' in the generating moments of this constitution' (Giddens, 1979, p. 5). Giddens (1991) does believe that, while there exists 'ontological security' that gives a 'sense of continuity and order in events', 'self' is not a passive entity, determined solely by external forces. In this manner, Giddens moves away from 'dualism' ('agent/agency' and 'structure/rules of resources' being viewed as the two distinctions) towards 'duality' where both agency and structure are viewed as a part of the same phenomenon (Ransome, 2010). Moreover, Giddens, in his book 'Modernity and Self-identity' (1991) highlighted that modernity features 'an interconnection between two extremes of extensionality and intentionality: globalising influences on one hand and personal dispositions on the other' (Giddens, 1991, p. 1). He therefore avoids an extreme positioning of extensionality (socially constructed identity or structure) and intentionality (personal identity or agency), and considers these positions to be two sides of the same coin.

Models of Scientific Identity 5

Our intention here is not to discuss further the various theoretical tension in relation to structure and agency identified by Block (2013) or Giddens, instead we are interested in exploring 'science identity' that is shaped by the internal individual agency. In this chapter we focus on young people's broad experiences and personal dispositions in relation to science education and career preferences, and highlight science identity-linked research models that explore the stability and fluidity of identity in shaping one's science identity. In doing that, we explore the influences that are derived from 'social agents', linking an individual's personal identity with the externally shaped 'global forces' of society such as social class, race, religion, ethnicity, gender, institutional status etcetera.

SOCIAL AGENTS

So who might be these social agents? By social agents we mean families, parents, peers, schools, teachers, churches, clerics, youth centres, youth workers, employment, and employers and many more besides. These are social agents that are situated – and that intercede – between individual agency and the larger social forces. In this section, we highlight some of the literature on the impact of parents, school science and science teachers on individuals' science identities that allow them to countenance a science-based education and career.

(i) Parents and Families

Numerous studies have identified parental involvement as an important ingredient in promoting academic success (for example: Jeynes, 2010; Seginer, 2006). In this vein, we note that parental influence varies on the basis of ethnicity, race, class, gender, etc. For example, Bourdieu and Passeron (1990) have indicated the importance of the:

> *disposition, which middle class students or middle rank teachers, and a fortiori, students whose fathers are middle rank teachers, manifest towards education (p. 192).*

In a similar vein, Gilmartin et al.'s (2006) research, conducted in Southern California working with 1126 tenth grade students (age 15-16), has reported on the importance of 'family science orientation' ('students' perception of family interest in and value of science'). In their case, this depends heavily on the family's ethnicity. In their work they have argued that Latino and Asian-American students' science career aspirations were strongly linked to perceptions of family support – rather more so than was the case for White and Black/African American students. They have suggested that the reasons for this difference in ethnicity/race are not clear but that, in Latino and Asian/American families, parents certainly seem to have considerable power and influence in family decision-making. Gilmartin et al. (2006) indicated that these parents commonly make very clear their likes and dislikes about routes to study and prospective career choices.

Archer et al.'s (2012, 2013, 2104) ASPIRES important work has used a strong Bourdieusian framework to indicate that a family's 'science capital' refers to science-related qualifications, understanding, knowledge (about science and 'how it works'), interest and social contacts (e.g., knowing someone who works in a science-related job). Their (2014) analysis indicates that young people's aspirations are:

> *not simply individual cognitions residing within children's heads, unaffected by their social contexts. Rather, children's aspirations and views of science careers are formed within families, and these families play an important, albeit complex, role in shaping the boundaries and nature of what children can conceive of as possible and desirable and the likelihood of their being able to achieve these aspirations (p. 902).*

They point out that those families with higher levels of science capital (a derivative of Bourdieu's social, cultural and economic capital) tend to be middle-class – although this is not always the case, and not all middle-class families necessarily possess that much science capital. For this reason, in

Models of Scientific Identity   7

their final analysis, they recommend that 'there is a strong case to be made for the implementation of strategies designed to increase science capital within the UK families, to help make science (and hence science aspirations) more 'known' and familiar within families' everyday lives' (p. 189). Archer et al. (2013) also indicate that the majority of the parents felt that:

> *science careers are associated with masculinity and held a perception of science as being an area that more men than women study and work in.... over half did view the sciences as dominated by men, although views differed considerably among parents as to the reasons for this imbalance, being divided between biological/genetic arguments and socio-cultural/structural arguments...' (p. 181).*

This sense of gender inequality was also seen by the students but not as intensely as by their parents.

Parental power has also been illustrated through Chinese parenting styles (Tao, 2016) – such as the concept of Chinese 'Tiger mother', which refers to mothers with very high power over their children's academic achievements. These mothers exert their power through setting explicit targets for their children, and expecting their children to attain the highest levels of achievement despite their ability range and the child's personal ambitions. In contrast, in the context of the USA, Ing (2014) noted that such external motivation driven by the parents tends to be short-lived and does little to help to push forward levels of attainment. For this reason, parents who generate intrinsic motivate in their children (Ing, 2014) achieve better, and generate greater student's persistence in a subject (in this case mathematics), than overtly extrinsic motivation. Jungert and Koestner (2015) also believe that parents should support students intrinsically in order to have a long-lasting effect. Moreover, as Hyde et al. (2016) point out, this relies upon effective communication (rather than one-way direction) between parent and the child about the future subject and career choices. To shade this slightly, Jungert and Koestner (2015) have reported that 'parental autonomy support' for high school students (age 15-16) was seen to be most helpful largely for students who already with 'an intrinsic disposition in a domain' (p. 376).

(ii) School Science and Science Literacy

From our perspective, it is quite clear that schools – and their school science curriculums – have considerable influence in mediating between home and wider social cultures. We believe the role of school science is vitally important. There is a considerable body of work addressing the nature and importance of school science itself (for example, Hulleman & Harackiewicz, 2009; Yeager & Walton, 2011), and the ways it influences science identity and students' aspirations towards future science education and career (Pike & Dunne, 2011). For example, Stuckey et al. (2013) see 'socio-scientific issues within science teaching' as highly relevant in the sense that classroom discussions of the societal dimension broadly influence perceptions of science and science education. The sense here is that students will have a positive attitude towards science if they can relate to daily-life science and 'real-life problem solving' (Mandler et al., 2012).

Beyond this, a positive influence of the school science curriculum means a positive view of 'science literacy for all'. Because the majority of the students will not (and cannot) become mainstream scientists, they can all, however, become science literate citizens (Hassard & Dias, 2009). This is recognised by many science educators as a worthwhile goal because they believe that pre-professional and established science is not as important as a broadly-based humanistic science-literate approach. As Archer et al. (2014) have emphasised in the context UK science education, the provision of scientific literacy and discussions of the nature of science (NoS) in the science classrooms, are important because:

> widening participation in STEM is not only beneficial for the STEM "pipeline" (the supply of professionals to work within STEM fields of employment) and the UK's economy, but also for increasing the scientific literacy of the general UK population. Both are desirable because scientific literacy is viewed as an important form of symbolic capital (Archer et al., 2014[a], p. 22).

Chapman and Feldman (2016) adapted their research from Carlone and Johnson (2007) and showed that student's active participation in school science – with a focus on enquiry-based science learning (EBL) and teaching – can be extremely fruitful in both establishing and polishing individuals' science identity. For this kind of reason, Osborne (2014) designed a model for school science based on 'scientific activity', his model being composed of three phases: 'investigation', 'evaluation' and 'developing explanations and solutions'. In addition to 'scientific investigation', Osborne (2014) also indicated the incorporation of literacy in teaching and learning science, of 'writing science, talking science, reading science, doing science and representing scientific ideas' (p. 188). In supporting his model, Osborne criticised general science classrooms for failing to give more importance to investigative laboratory work that incorporates enquiry based teaching and learning. Moreover, he recommended that mathematics should act as a 'core feature' to incorporate NoS in the science classrooms and stated that 'avoiding the opportunity to use mathematical forms and representations is a failure to build students competency to make meaning in science' (Osborne, 2014, p. 187).

Nevertheless, MacDonald (2014) points out that such attempts to make school science sufficiently aspiring for students have failed. In this respect, Archer et al. (2014) also lament the fact that, 'despite the rhetoric of scientific literacy for all students, science in schools remains virtually unchanged; students are confronted with basic facts and theories' (p. 5). Similarly, Hassard and Dias (2009) chide science teachers for emphasising too heavily the 'science content objectives (traditional approach) as compared to NoS and application objectives (humanistic approach)' (p 45). These critiques and suggestions indicate that it is important to develop (i) scientific literacy for all (ii) students' personal science aspirations and appreciate (iii) students' cultural diversity in the classroom.

(iii) Science Teachers

Archer and DeWitt (2016) see the role of the science teacher as one of the main social agents in helping students to identify themselves as people for whom 'science is for me'. Teachers, MacDonald (2014) says, play a vital role in nourishing the individual agency of a student – rather than simply labelling students in terms of ethnicity, gender, academic achievement and so on. Like Reid and McCallum (2014), she recommends that:

teachers and schools must engage in discussions with students about their aspirations to consider how their learning connects with significant people and places in their communities (p. 205).

However, not all science teachers manage this level of engagement and, more generally, the school system in the UK, as in many other places, fails to incorporate cultural diversity and equality (Hattam and Zipin, 2009) within discussions of science careers. To tackle these issues, Elmesky and Seiler (2007) suggested that the fundamental requirement is to generate successful social interactions through a positive emotional climate in the science classroom – a climate, they say, that is key to establishing individuated science identity. In a similar vein, Lewis (2008) recommends that science educators, schools and teachers:

give emotions the same status as cognitions. Just as cognitions can lead to emotions, emotions can lead to cognitions. The theory implies no status difference (p. 745).

In this light, Hampden-Thompson and Bennett (2013) found the effect of emotions in altering science engagement to be quite obvious – particularly where teachers cater for these aspects, these 'triggers', in the classroom. This is because they believe that, when a student's inner sense of self (self-schema) comes in contact with the field of science within a positive science classroom, this leads to nurtured emotional energy which, in turn, results in an approving emergent identity. Lock et al. (2013) report that students with a positive science identity (in their case physics identity) believe that their physics teacher sees them – and treats them – as a 'physics person'. On the other hand, negative emotions (fear, anger, lack of focus, failing tests) can result in a 'hardening of cultural boundaries' (Carambo, 2015, p. 161), when for example a student's inner 'sense of self is disrespected' by the teachers and/or school. As Kane (2012) and MacDonald (2014, p. 6) have pointed out, 'teachers often have lower (stereotypical) expectations of under-represented groups in STEM reinforcing their non-STEM identity'.

From what we have said so far, we see science teachers as having a duty to (i) see and respect their students as individuals rather than differentiating and grouping them on the basis of perceived biological differences, (ii) capture the essence of the student as (potentially) a sciencey person, and (iii) nurture classroom environments by incorporating positive emotions and aspirations towards science education and future career choices. There are numerous other possible solutions that have been researched in association with science teachers, such as addressing the lack of specialist teachers (for example, Taylor, 2009), providing support and training (for example, the UK's House of Commons Children, Schools and Families Committee, 2010), encouraging the appropriate use of teaching resources (Beauchamp & Parkinson, 2008; Wood & Ashfield, 2008; Tissenbaum et al., 2012) – and remedying many other 'improper' teaching practices – over which we draw a veil in this chapter.

MODELS OF IDENTITY

So far, we have acknowledged the power of global forces, broad social structures, and seen how these might shape young people through the actions of many of the social agents in their immediate zones of activity. We now move to consider the stability and change of individual identities and the nature of a core identity. We set out our stall at the start of the chapter: from our own research (Salehjee & Watts, 2015, Salehjee, 2017) we see clear indications of stability in science identity (fixed propensities both for and against science). Between these 'poles of fixity', we also see degrees of fluidity, where young people are yet to consolidate their thoughts and opinions, and remain relatively open to being a 'sciencey person'. We offer some cases of this in action towards the end of the chapter. There are many, though, who would challenge this view of a stability and/or fluidity at the core of people's identity.

We divide the discussion to follow in two ways: first to consider the challenge that there is no stability to identity, that individuals are chameleon-like and present different identities in different social situations, that the situational context determines the facet of identity being presented. Second we consider the challenge that, whether there is stability or not, it is (global) structural social forces that dominate in the formation of identity, and not the individual's (core) personal agency and dispositions.

(i) Discussions of Stability

Writers like Gee (2000), Carlone and Johnson (2007) and Brickhouse and Potter (2011) indicate that identities are not fixed at any point and, instead, develop over time in response to particular social contexts. The primary social agents recognized by Gee and Carlone and Johnson mainly include institutions (school, science industries), teachers, peers/faculty members and government agencies. This approach acts to preclude – or at least minimize – the individual agency that we believe is important.

We begin with Gee (2000) who uses the term 'socially situated identity' to illustrate the multiple identities people adopt in different practices and contexts, and argues that identity can be viewed in four different modes:

(i) *Nature-identity*, which refers to a state developed from what we have termed 'global forces'. Gee believes that identity provided by 'nature' lies outside the control of individuals and gives an example of an 'African American' label, which he believes can be understood as being a biological construct

Models of Scientific Identity

(ii) *Institution-identity*, a position controlled by authorities within institutions. Here Gee indicates a form of identity where the control of institutions overshadows individuality. For example, a passport number, national health number, employment payroll number, military assignation or a 'prisoner number' can be used to 'institutionally identify' people

(iii) *Discourse-identity*, where an individual trait is recognised through discourse/dialogue with 'rational' social agents such as schools, teachers, youth workers and governments. 'Passive discourse identity' is an act of acquiescence by the individual; whereas 'active discourse identity' exhibits some form of control over this, though largely to please others in order to achieve something better in life. An example might be an individual making false claims on his or her inability to work due to poor health conditions in order to receive public funding from the government

(iv) *Affinity-identity*, which refers to the experiences shared in the practice of 'affinity groups'. For example, according to Gee (2000, p. 100), African American people could identify themselves in relation to their 'participation in certain practices' (p. 109). Involvement and sharing with these groups shape strong personal agency in developing personal and group identities.

That is, Gee's (2000) sense of identity is guided principally by social agents and agencies such as institutes, schools, families and groups of people, peers etcetera. The four modes above serve to 'enact' the global forces (ethnicity, race, etc.) in shaping one's identity. He defines self-identification only as 'the kind of person one is seeking to be and enact in the here and now' (p. 13). In this respect, Gee rejects a *definitive* core of identity, not least because any such core is never fully formed – or always has a tendency to change.

Carlone and Johnson (2007) have extended Gee's viewpoints on identity directly into science education, to present three science identity trajectories: (i) *competence* ('knowledge and understanding of science content'), (ii) *performance* ('social performances of relevant scientific practices'), and (iii) recognition (recognising oneself and getting recognised by others'). They do give some acknowledgement to a degree of personal agency in that they incorporate some individual identification of competence, performance and recognition. They argue, though, that identities are not built in isolation and state that 'identity arises out of the constraints and resources available in the local setting' (p. 1192), for example through families, career counsellors and institutions.

These authors' classic work on 'understanding the science experiences of successful women of color' was published in 2007 and involved a longitudinal research for six years to establish the practical grounds of science identity in women. Their analysis developed three science identity trajectories that interacted the global forces of ethnicity, race and gender with social agents such as university faculty members. Their first category is that of 'research scientists', where the participants themselves – as well as the science faculty members – identify them as 'sciencey people'. The second category were females with 'altruistic science identity' somewhat similar to Gee's (2000) 'nature identity'; the participants felt science to be an integral part of their 'genetic makeup' and, in addition, were recognised by others as sciencey 'women of colour'. The last category emerged as 'disrupted scientist identity', where the participants were not recognised as 'sciencey' by the others. Although these women were successful in their scientific careers, they were largely excluded from being 'science people' in terms of gender, ethnicity and racial factors. So, despite their 'disrupted scientist identity', women, black and other ethnic communities can, and do, survive and retain some science identity. In a later paper, Johnson et al. (2011) acknowledged that successful women of colour have succeeded in science careers through working harder than white male peers (with similar or even with less ability) to achieve recognition. Therefore these 'disrupted scientists' succeeded in their science careers by avoiding negative identities attached to them by others, and by putting themselves in a place where gender/racial identity can successfully intersect with science identity.

From this perspective, Carlone and Johnson take their influences directly from Gee (2000). For example, they state that while 'cultural

Models of Scientific Identity 15

production' allows the 'possibility of the women transforming meanings of "science people" and what it means to be a woman of colour' (p. 1192), in actuality their female participants 'were not free to develop any kind of science identity'. This indicates a considerable reliance on the fixity of broad global forces and social agents in the system.

Brickhouse et al. (2000) discuss different 'kinds of people'. They point to students who 'forge identities in communities of practice' (p. 443), and they take the view that identity is certainly not 'stable or single' (p. 443) – that a person can be actively involved in different communities of practice at the same time and identify as a different person in each case. Within this, there are some 'kinds of people' who are positive in adopting scientific explanations, interpretations, understanding, and who exhibit strong engagement with science. Similarly, Kelman (2006) defines identity by saying that 'an individual accepts influence from another person or a group in order to establish or maintain a satisfying self-defining relationship to the other' (p. 3). In addition, people accept and/or decline certain decisions to please a particular social agent or a group, in order to achieve certain reward (or approval) and avoid punishment (or disapproval) from other (s).

Unlike Gee and Carlone and Johnson, though, Brickhouse et al. (2000) do give some credence to stability of identity in their discussions. They adopt Lave and Wenger's (1991) 'identity in practice' as a means of discussing transformation in the process of learning. They illustrate this by addressing the global forces experienced by one of their students, Ruby (Brickhouse & Potter, 2001). They describe how Ruby's African American heritage had a significant impact on her movement from a suburban middle school to an urban high school. The central feature of Ruby's story is that, in order to transform her African American girl identity, she needed to challenge and overcome negative self-perceptions (for example: African American girls' restricted identity). Ruby broke the norms of feminism and African American identity by choosing to interact in school with a wide crossection of people from a variety of ethnic and gendered backgrounds. She rejected the easy route of simply being a stereotypical black girl in the school. From this example, Brickhouse and Potter (2001) illustrate a duality model where personal constructions of identity work in concert with other people's (peers, teachers and parents) perceptions of ethnicity and gender related to that individual.

While there are many cases where people 'go along with prevailing forces', there are numerous other examples of people who 'go against the grain' as Archer et al. (2014[b]) note. For instance, Amal – a thirteen year-old female student in a chemistry lesson (Salejhee, Ludhra & Watts, 2018) – is not only enthusiastic about separating chlorophyll (pigment) colours on a chromatogram in chemistry, she also describes herself as a person who loves chemistry even in a non-school context indicating a 'kind of person who understands the world scientifically'. This identity stays with her and exhibits a form of Giddens's 'ontological security' over time. 'Being sciencey', though, may not be sustained outside of the school classroom or community. So, in contrast, another student (Fiza), with similar enthusiasm within the lesson, might identify herself to her peers outside the school science laboratory as a person who 'hates chemistry' (Salehjee, Ludhra & Watts, 2018). We see something of this at the individual level: not all children within a 'high science capital family' will aspire to a future in science and some will 'rebel'. Equally, some within a 'low science capital family' do find a route into science. Moreover, in a separate paper, Brickhouse and Potter (2001) go on to recommend that teachers and schools have a responsibility to address the issues of diversity and identity in classrooms and to provide clear opportunities and space for students' individual identity constructions in relation to their multicultural backgrounds.

(ii) Increasing Degrees of Personal Autonomy

Hazari et al. (2015) followed Carlone and Johnson's (2007) model using the three dimensions of recognition, performance and competence, initially based on Gee's identity construct. Here, these authors are critical of Gee's (2000) emphasis on external recognition and his neglect of individual agency control – in particular, the role of personal thoughts,

Models of Scientific Identity 17

emotions, cognition and learning. Therefore, to further incorporate greater individuality, they added a fourth dimension of 'interest' in their model. They consider this to be 'critically relevant in influencing the decision of who and what a student wants to be?' (Hazari et al., 2010, p. 982). We understand interest here as a verb that exhibits individual agency, one that shapes one's preferences, choices and/or decisions. Moreover, Hazari et al. believe 'performance, perceptions of competence, the perception of others, and interest all influence a focal construct' (p. 998) in developing – in their case – 'physics identity'. To this extent, they believe that students with physics identity have a strong desire to enter into careers in physics. Their work also included testing different teaching strategies to promote physics identity in female students, where they found a strategy of 'discussion on under-representation of women in physics' to be significant enough to foster physics identity in female students (Hazari et al., 2013). Their sense is that teachers and educators need to cater for individual students' cultural identities in the science classrooms. Moreover, Lock, Hazari and Potwin (2013) maintain that the key contributors towards physics career choices involve recognition of the 'interest dimensions' of students' science identity trajectories. Hazari et al. (2013) also suggest that physics identity can be developed through the mediation of social agents with an emphasis on teachers and teaching strategies. In these instances we see, in comparison to Gee (2000) and Carlone and Johnson (2007), that Hazari and her colleagues are inclined more towards individual agency than global forces. Their dimension of recognition involves both self-recognition and recognition by others; moreover the aspect of 'interest' is quite individually-centered.

Carlone and Johnson's (2007) work is also evident in Kane's (2012) study of *competence*, *performance* and *recognition*. In his empirical research he included students' self-narrated interviews involving 'their experiences in school and science with their performances of self in the midst of complex, spontaneous classroom engagements with their peers and teacher' (p. 457). Kane's work (2012) highlights such ingredients to the individual agency as interest, self-confidence, self-ability and understanding of self as a good student. These factors were found to be of different degrees and were valued differently by the students themselves, their peers and their teachers. In making recommendations to educators and teachers, Kane believes that, for African American children for example, identities need to be given special corrective attention because teachers and wider society often do not take students' individual competence, performance and recognition into consideration and, rather, it sees such learners as being 'at risk'. Moreover, Kane (2012) and Rodrigues (2014) have suggested the need to appreciate the multicultural diversity that students bring to science classrooms – and to change the culture in order to prevent the marginalisation of so-called stigmatised groups. Kane (2012) also suggested that educators need to consider the multiple identities of individuals not only as science students, but as overall students, for example, where a 'brainy' student might position himself/herself within a 'sciencey' group. Therefore, Kane (2012) emphasises individuality alongside the impact of social agents in developing science identities – in this case, in African American children. In our opinion, Kane, like Brickhouse before him, believes that social agents (schools, teachers, peers and educators more generally) 'enact' global forces in shaping science identity.

Going further, Robnett et al. (2015) view 'identity as a scientist' as a core component of an individual's identity. They also acknowledge the work by Estrada et al. (2010) by arguing that there will be some students, though not all, who will continue with science studies because of positive exposure to academic science, not least through – say – science outreach programmes. In this vein, they give considerable emphasis to individuals deciding who they are and with which communities of practice they wish to participate, and less emphasis on the communities deciding the individual's position in society. Like Hazari and her colleagues (2015), 'interest' features strongly, and Robnett et al. (2015) argue for self-efficacy that acts as a mediator between positive science research experiences and science identity. They understand 'science self-efficacy' to originate from sources such as 'mastery experiences' and vicarious (mediated) learning which they see as being prominent, particularly within undergraduates.

Models of Scientific Identity 19

However, these authors have also reported that the association between 'research experience', 'science self-efficacy' and 'identity as a scientist' – showed little if any significant differences in relation to gender and ethnicity. They did indicate, though, that students from over-represented ethnic backgrounds (Asian American or European American) exhibited 'more variance in identity as a scientist' as compared to students from underrepresented ethnic backgrounds (African American, Latino or Native American). We take from this that Robnett et al. (2015) are further inclined towards individual agency than others we have discussed so far. So, while external forces, such as outreach programmes do enhance an individual's experience and willingness to engage with science, self-efficacy is centrally important in filling the gap between positive science experiences and science identity.

(iii) Global Social Structures are Dominant?

In science education, Archer and her colleagues (2010; 2013; 2016) have extended the work of Bourdieu on identity and developed the term 'science identity'. Bourdieu's work has been widely used in identity-based research and 'the two key constructs fundamental to Bourdieu's understanding of structure and agency are *habitus* and *field'* (Block, 2013, p. 136). The habitus provides space where agents act in a specific 'field' or context, utilising *capital* or resources (economic, cultural, social or symbolic). Broadly, Bourdieu (1986) describes three main types of capital: economic, social and cultural. Economic capital involves goods, money and could be institutionalised in property rights, which Bourdieu believes to be the basis of the other capitals. Social capital is described as 'the aggregate of actual or potential resources linked to possessions of a durable network of essentially institutionalised relationships of mutual acquaintance and recognition' (Bourdieu, 1986, p. 248). In other words, it involves social obligations or connections that can be converted into economic capital. Cultural capital exists in the following three states:

(i) *Embodied*: It is the state in which the habitus (individual dispositions) is quite automatic and pre-reflexive and does not involve conscious control. Any possible change or transformation of this state is quite limited (Claussen & Osborne, 2012). An embodiment relates to something that is learned in life and emerges in different occasions as an automatic response/action. Here we understand 'embodied' as a construct of individuality because Bourdieu (1990) stated that the embodied state 'is an active subject confronting society as if society were an object constituted externally' (p. 70)

(ii) *Objectified*: This is the state that 'takes the form of cultural goods (pictures, books, dictionaries, instruments) and can easily be transmitted in its materiality. However, this form requires embodied capital to fully appreciate and use it beneficially' (Claussen and Osborne, 2012, p. 62). Certain cultural goods can be of benefit and can reach the embodied state. That said, not all the students will actually turn out to be scientists with all the essential cultural goods and with an understanding of the value of becoming a scientist

(iii) *Institutionalised*: which resemble Gee's (2000) institutional identity. Institutions provide 'a certificate of cultural competence which confers on its holder a conventional, constant, legally guaranteed value with respect to culture' (Bourdieu, 1986, p. 50). Here the emphasis is on social agencies like schools to reward and enhance the person's credentials

Jenkins (1992) and DiMaggio (1982) criticised Bourdieu's concept of habitus as being deterministic, with insufficient emphasis on consciousness and agency. King (2000) believes that, while Bourdieu did acknowledge subjectivism with objectivism in regards to meaning-making processes, he also saw that:

> *Bourdieu has failed to take his own greatest insight seriously, and he has slipped into the very objectivism whose poverty he has done so much to highlight'* (p. 431).

Models of Scientific Identity

Sullivan (2002) has been more scathing, in that 'Bourdieu's theory has no place not only for the individual agency but even individual consciousness' (p. 163). Sullivan also criticised Bourdieu's distinction and strength of cultural capital over other forms of capital (social, economic) as being unclear. Moreover, Erel (2010) indicated that 'Bourdieu has rarely explored how forms of capital are activated for resistant purposes' (p. 647). Block (2013) has been more generous, in seeing that 'Bourdieu constantly navigated the line between determining the social structure and individual agency in his work spanning some 40 years' (p. 136).

In their extensive work in science education, Archer and her colleagues (Archer et al., 2010) lay the root causes of girls', and young people of low socio-economic status', non-participation in science as lying largely outside of the girls themselves (Archer et al., 2014[b]). They have used the idea of Bourdieu's capitals in science education and referred to this as 'science capital' – which deals with 'science related qualifications, understanding, knowledge, interest and social contacts' (p. 3). Their three main forms of science capital are as follows:

(i) Science linked to social/symbolic capital (for example: gender, ethnicity, social class, science communicated in social networks; interacting and/or idealising people with scientific knowledge and/or science related jobs)

(ii) Science linked to cultural capital (for example: science qualifications, scientific literacy, and understanding about nature of science)

(iii) Science linked to economic capital (for example: money to gain science capital and opportunities like visiting events and science centres) (Archer & Dewitt, 2016).

Archer and her colleagues also come subject to the same criticism as discussed above in regards to Bourdieu's work itself. In this form, Archer et al.'s (2014) science capital resembles an over-riding argument that identity as a sense of self is predominantly socially constructed within social settings (Spillane, 2000), and resembles an outcome of dialectical engagement with practical social activity, rather than being an innate property of individuals (Roth, 2007). In addition, Archer et al. have also been critiqued for their derivation of science capital from the cultural capital. As Claussen and Osborne (2012) indicate, it is not clear whether Archer's science capital is intrinsically justified or it dominates because of socio-historical contexts. Jensen and Wright (2015) have been critical, too, in that they see science capital to be distinct from cultural capital – Bourdieu's approach is to offer a much broader range of concepts that foster social mobility in an inherently unjust socio-cultural system. This is much more than 'science capital' can manage. Moreover, like Bourdieu, the 'field' identified by Archer et al. (2015[b]) affecting the struggle over science capital is unclear.

(iv) A Return to Individuality and Transformational Change

We began this chapter in the clear belief that there is a clear role for individual agency, the propensity for a student to identify him- or herself as a science person – without the necessity to resort to discussions of science capital (social, cultural, economic). There is a very long literature related to the nature of individualised identity in relation to agency and in relation to the others. Erikson (1973) called people 'in-groupers' and 'out-groupers'. While this can be understood of teenagers in terms, say, of skin colour, or cultural backgrounds that could lead to self-labelling (stereotyping), self-beliefs and self-identifying people, it can also be seen in their alliance with or against science and scientists, as 'people like me'. Erikson views identity formation to be successful and stable when one identifies who he/she is, who he/she wants to be within himself/herself, and who he/she wants to be in a particular social context.

Knud Illeris (2014) acknowledges Erikson's work. He links identity to Jack Mezirow's theory of transformational learning, as he believes that 'the concept of transformative learning comprises all learning that implies a change in the identity of the learner' (Illeris, 2014, p. 40). Illeris views identity transformation in a similar vein to Mezirow (1990, 2009). He

Models of Scientific Identity 23

explicates two main terms in his theory, first is 'meaning schemes', which are 'set of related and habitual expectations governing if-then, cause and effect, and category relationships as well as event sequences' (Mezirow, 1990, p. 2). Second is 'meaning perspectives', which are 'broad sets of predispositions resulting from psycho-cultural assumptions, which determine the horizons of our expectations' (Mezirow, 1991). His (2000) writing explores 'frames of reference' that encompass 'structures of culture and language through which we construe meaning by attributing coherence and significance to our experience' (Mezirow, 2009, p. 92).

Such frames elaborate the continuing conflicts in daily life that lead to the 'learning of new frames of reference' and eventually leading to self-development (D'Amato & Krasny, 2011). A frame of reference consists of 'two dimensions – habits of mind and resulting points of view' (Mezirow, 2009, p. 92). Habits of mind constitute a specific way of individual's thinking or feeling that results in a set of codes, and specific habits of mind result in specific 'points of view' as an awareness through, belief, sustained as a memory and/or attitude, the way of judging future related actions (Mezirow, 2009). For example, gender discrimination acting as a code can result in a point of view that science is 'not for me, because I am a girl'. This belief can remain in one's perception as a memory that, later in life, acts as a judgement/decision for not choosing science subjects in the future. Mezirow's theory sees identity to be fluid and subject to transformation but – at the same time – maintains that fluidity depends on some form of a disorienting dilemma, a possible dramatic life experience leading to transformation. As Mezirow (1978) states '...to negotiate the process of perspective transformation can be painful and treacherous... [one's] sense of identity and integrity...' can be challenged (p. 11) leading to transformed behaviours, feelings, beliefs, identity (Mezirow, 1991) values, attitudes, and perceptions (Jackson, 1986).

The primary link between Mezirow's theory and Illeris's (2014) identity model includes the 'meaning-making' process whereby individuals negotiate their understanding of self that shapes (transforms) their identity in certain social or cultural contexts. With similar intentions, Abes et al. (2007) introduced a 'meaning-making filter' as one of the main parts of their identity model in order to elaborate, extend or even transform the 'meaning-making capacity integrated' (p. 7) into a person's self-perceptions. This chimes with Mezirow's suggestion that transformational learning incorporates the 'making of meanings', and he describes the process as an intense, thoughtful journey of constructing the meaning of oneself through life experiences. The meaning-making process in a person's learning depends upon critical self-reflection on the experiences that have taken place within a particular context.

At first, a person's life experiences (rather than typical academic learning) act as the key initiators of change, and these depend on the varying contexts and time at which the life changing experiences are practiced (Mezirow et al., 2009). These contextual life experiences have been visualised by Abes et al. (2007) in their 're-conceptualized model of multiple dimensions of identity' where 'a person experiences (his or) her life, such as family, sociocultural conditions, and current experiences' (p. 3). It is quite clear that not all the contextual influences/life experiences will be life-changing, and Illeris (2014) makes the case that life experiences (and/or influences) need to be of 'higher order' and require considerable energy to create changes – especially if those changes interfere with strong pre-held affiliations towards something. These 'life changing transformational experiences' which includes events, triggers and interventions initiate 'discourse leading to critical examination of normative assumptions underpinning the learners … value judgments or normative expectations' (Mezirow 2000, p. 31). Such discourse elements lead to self-examination of pre-held assumptions, and are catered through dialogue with self and with others. Dialogue allows people to critically reflect on the contextual influences, and these evaluations require a 'critical and reflective lens to authenticate their reasons to adapt new actions' (Mezirow, 1996, p. 162). Through dialogue, one can determine the boundary that accepts or rejects certain life experience through 'continuous effort to negotiate contented meaning' (Mezirow, 2000, p. 3). When this meaning system is found to be inadequate in accommodating some life experience, it can be replaced with a new meaning perspective that exhibits change in habits of the mind, one that is 'more inclusive, discriminating, open, emotionally capable of change, and reflective'; in other words, more developed' (Mezirow, 2000, p. 7) which results in transforming points of view.

We believe that, for some people, a complete transformation in their meaning perspectives is possible and can happen. For example, there are numerous accounts of people undergoing life-changing events – after a significant illness or disability, a significant change in relationships, a major shift of occupation, and so on. For some people smaller life changes might have a higher impact in choosing science or non-science discipline. For example, a love for physics (in general) at school might later occupy meaning of one's life after meeting a rocket scientist. Although, Mezirow's theory has been challenged for its individualistic mode of analysis, with few links to social action (Welton, 1995; Kegan, 2009).

In our view, this places Mezirow's theory principally within an individuated 'intentionality identity' rather than an extensionality 'global forces' approach. With Jarvis (2013), we view individuals as 'people' and their personality relates to the way they learn from the external culture. Jarvis believes that learning can be a 'lifelong process intrinsic to the living organism itself, whereby the individual internal life force experiences externality (through body and mind) and generates a permanent state of becoming in the human being' (2013, p. 13). His 'internal life force' is the force derived from individuality and, in turn, identity then interacts with externality leading to identity formation; therefore Jarvis applies both intentionality (IIA) and external extensional forces (GF) to the construct of identity. The idea of 'being itself' resembles Abes et al.'s (2007) idea of core and 'externality meaning', when an individual is exposed to contextual influences. Jarvis also indicates the fluid nature of the person's learning processes, which eventually form an identity. Within this view of learning, Jarvis (2009) has criticised Mezirow's theory because it focuses mainly on adults, creating a gap between adult and children's learning, and fails to relate Jarvis's sense of lifelong learning as a whole. In contrast, Jarvis (2009) believes that it is not always the meaning-making process that transforms learning – it can be daily life experiences that can be transformed by learning.

Illeris (2014) views identity transformation in a similar way to Mezirow, and has stated that 'the concept of transformative learning comprises all learning that implies a change in the identity of the learner' (p. 40). In addition, Illeris (2014) believes that 'identity involves learners' mental whole' (p. 39) and the important changes within person's mental whole can be taken as transformation that leads to alter one's identity in a way that we want ourselves and others to identify us (Illeris, 2014). Illeris has been critical of Mezirow's use of 'meaning perspectives and frames of reference', as being dominated by cognitive rather than affective learning. In answer to this critique, Mezirow recognised the importance of affective phenomena and believes that a frame of reference can have 'cognitive, conative and affective' functioning–consciously or unconsciously (Mezirow, 2009, p. 92). Even then, Illeris (2014) stated that while Mezirow (2000) links and understands emotions at the same time 'he understand emotions as a kind of concomitant or even distracting phenomenon in relation to what the real transformation is about, which is precisely meaning perspectives, frames of reference or as here our beliefs' (Illeris, 2014, p. 36).

Unlike Erikson (1982), Mezirow (2000) and Illeris (2014) are not certain that identity is constructed within the time frame of adolescence – and actually believe that transformation cannot *really* occur at the early stage of 'teenage'. While Illeris (2014) concedes that episodes of provisional identity might emerge in the early ages (even before the age of thirteen) and can form 'long lasting effect on identity' (p. 124), Mezirow (2000) believes that transformation is fully prominent in adults. Illeris's (2014) view is that identity development mainly takes place after adolescence and, therefore, after the compulsory age of school (science) education from ages 11 -16 years.

We believe that age, and the intensity of the triggers that might lead to a life-changing experience, vary among people even from within the same cultural, social and economic backgrounds. Such triggers could be planned to some extent (through outreach programs, meeting scientists and/or science community interventions to inspire students towards science). Or

Models of Scientific Identity 27

they might be accidental. An example of the accidental trigger could be 'trees', as Loehle (2010) has stated:

> *Some individuals find themselves fascinated with ants or birds or fossils from a young age. Why? I have never seen an explanation for this early attraction to a scientific subject. For me it was trees. I can remember the trees in the neighbourhood where I lived at age 7 so well I can still tell you what species they were and how tall (p. 13).*

Another example of an accidental trigger could be the death of a younger sibling that transformed the decision of a business student to become a child specialist. A planned trigger could be when a teacher designs a particular visit to a hospital (in one of the deprived areas in their country X) to incorporate students role as citizens. At the hospital, students came to know that – due to the lack of child specialists in their country – there are high mortality rates of children under the age of seven. This planned intervention along with a series of other planned interventions might transform some of the 'non-sciencey' students towards becoming a child specialist, a nurse, a laboratory technician or even someone who wants to build a children's hospital in country X.

Archer et al. (2012, 2013, and 2015) indicate such triggers to be linked with 'science capitals' involving resources such as parents, schools, and teachers. Abes et al. (2007) call these contextual influences, Illeris (2014) described them as 'conditions', and Mezirow (2000) sees them as 'experiences' leading to disorienting dilemmas. But, at the same time, from the above discussion based on self-identity subject to transformation, depends on the stability and fluidity of identity. When young adults are asked what subjects they will choose at A-level, they take time to answer and give their decision. This entails some kind of stable core that gives them positive and negative signals, where some students might take longer than others, where their identity is quite fluid and the core is challenged by both enjoyable and unpleasant experiences.

The stability of core identities is always in question. It could be that the transformation takes place gradually as Heddy and Pugh (2015, p. 56) believe: that 'transformative experiences may be a way to facilitate micro changes in students that, when accumulated, lead to transformative outcomes'. Nohl (2015) argues that transformation need not necessarily start with a disorienting dilemma – it can start 'unnoticed, incidentally, and sometimes even casually, when a new practice is added to old habits' (p. 45) or, even sometimes, the process of transformation starts with great emotional experiences but then later the processes fail or even the new meaning-making process does not challenge the pre-held disorienting dilemma. People with 'fluid' science identities can – potentially – be more open to accidental and/or planned transformative interventions and widen their options, exhibiting transformation.

We now examine Illeris's (2014) and Abes's et al. (2007) models of identity to discuss two prominent models of identity and identity transformations as mentioned above.

(v) Illeris's Model of Identity

As noted above, Illeris's (2014) general structure of identity belongs within a framework of intentionality (IIA). His model exhibits a three-layered structure of identity that includes a core identity, personality layer and preference layer (Figure 1).

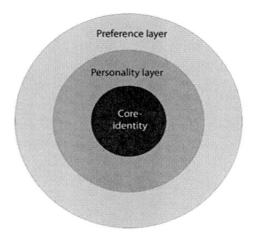

Figure 1. The general structure of identity (Illeris, 2014, p. 71).

Models of Scientific Identity 29

Illeris termed the inner most-layer the 'core', the most stable and solid layer that controls the construction of the subsequent layers. He believes that the core identity is developed and extended during childhood by elements such as gender; family identity, etc. and that change in the core is quite gradual unless it experiences a life changing event. Surrounding the core is the 'personality layer' where transformation is primarily apparent. Illeris (2014) believes that this layer includes 'who and how the individual wants to be and appears in relation to others and the surrounding world' (p. 72). This layer is susceptible to change 'in connection to important experiences, events, exchange of views and similar kind of interactions' (Illeris, 2014, p. 73). The impact of exchanges of views and social interactions resemble Gee's (2000) 'affinity identity', which is experienced through shared practices with 'elite' groups of people. This allows for free will in choosing a particular group to which an individual is attached. Rodogno (2012) describes this as 'attachment identity' (and is a 'deep' understanding of a notion of identity) that relies on expressions such as 'caring about', 'of importance', 'attachment to' and 'what matters to me'. That is, it is an identity ultimately anchored in a person's attachments. Again Gee (2000) emphasises the free will exercised in choosing the group in accordance to the 'kind of person they are' (p. 106) – it is a freedom that might be restricted for those who 'lack access, networking and mobility' (p. 121).–Illeris's outermost layer is the preference layer, where the individual chooses and acts without entailing too much effort (thinking, feeling or acting). The changes in the conditions (daily life activities) being experienced in this layer are somewhat independent of self-perceptions and involve minimal energy to make any change: 'whether we in the situation to have the energy to make such changes ... [they] do not mean much to us, and we have long ago got used to the idea that we shall be open and ready for change' (Illeris, 2014, p. 73-74).

This identity model gives a general structure that exhibits the possibility of identity transformation interlinking both one's core identity and out-facing personality. It serves both external and internal forces and, in relation to external forces, involves an individual's participation, dialogue and/or discourse with social, cultural and/or economic 'capitals' or resources that can be linked to the personality layer. Illeris's (2014) core identity empowers the personality layer, which is more susceptible to transformation (through a conscious understanding of self in relation to others) than the core. Robnett et al. (2015) and Illeris emphasise the stability of core identity as being dominant over influences from others and surroundings. It is only very limited and strong life changing events that have the ability to transform the core identity. Robnett (2015) refers 'being a scientist' as part of the core component of identity construct.

In addition to the general structure above in Figure 1, Illeris (2014) extended his identity model to involve different 'part identities' such as work identity, family identity, everyday identity, etc. (Figure 2). He believes this transverse model of part identities to be interlinked with the central identity (including core, personality layer and preference layer) and each different part identity comprises of all the three layers identified as well. The idea of part identities working simultaneously is an appealing notion, because an individual can utilise part of – say – his or her work identity with cultural identity, etc. Moreover, a person acts and reacts differently to different situations and the activation of various identities is evident when trying to accomplish different roles (Burke & Stets, 2009). So, in this case a particular identity (surrounding the central identity) can switch on/off due to the exposure to different situations, influences and/or experiences. And this switching on and off process might later affect the central identity. Therefore, Illeris's (2014) model of part identities combined GF (extensionality) and IIA (intentionality) ideologies resulting in a composite model (Figure 2).

It is important here to note a few limitations to Illeris' model. First, in connection with his preference layer, Illeris is inexact about the everyday conditions that have an ability to transform parts of the personality layer and that might even transform the core. As Illeris (2014) himself believes, the boundary between the personality layer and preference layer is unclear. Our sense of remedy here is to suggest a 'controlling filter' between the personality layer and preference layer. We see this controlling filter as a filter that controls the conscious conditions (like Kane's (2012) contested spaces) and/or objects (like Bourdieu's objects), a filter that permits or rejects the opposing conditions/objects. This permission or rejection is based on the intensity of the conditions in relation to the automatic dispositions (embodied).

Second, while Illeris's (2014) transverse model does give an insight to part identities surrounding the central identity, again, the interlinking between one form of the outer structure identity to the central or to another form of identity seems unduly complex. It seems to be extraordinarily difficult to link the different identities to the central identity. For example, it is not straightforward to understand how Illeris's (2014) 'work identity' in its own orbit surrounds the core, personality and preference layers because, in this particular situation, work might not be of over-riding concern for the individual. But then, nor did 'work identity' fit in the preference layer, and so linking 'work identity' to the central three layered identity might prove difficult to adapt.

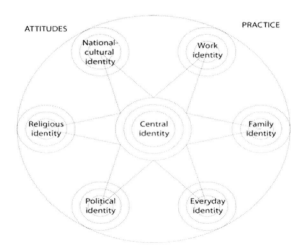

Figure 2. An example of part identity structure (Illeris, 2014, p. 76).

(vi) Models of Multiple Dimensions

Unlike Illeris's (2014) transverse identity, Jones and McEwen's (2000) model appears less complex in terms of picturing one core surrounding the multiple identities. Moreover, this model provides a distinction between multiple identities and contextual influences and, in our opinion, the presence of contextual influences provides an open space to capture social influences/triggers – a space that is lacking in Illeris's (2014) general model. Jones and McEwen (2000) describe identity theories as 'representing the on-going construction of identities and the influence of changing contexts on the experience of identity development' (p. 408). They propose a conceptual model (Figure 3), where they argue that there are two general parts to an 'identity' construct:

(i) The outer contextual layer includes influences from family background, socio-cultural conditions, current experiences, career choices, etc. The intersecting circles termed as identity dimensions placed around the core identity and within the premises of contextual ring. Moreover, the intensity of the 'relative salience of these identity dimensions is indicated by dots located on each of the identity dimension circles' (Jones and McEwen, 2000, p. 410). These include self-perceived dimensions such as gender, culture, faith, class, etc.

(ii) The central core, which includes the 'inner personal identity' that we have for ourselves. This resembles Illeris (2014) core identity.

Later, in 2007, this model of multiple dimension of identity (MMDI) was reconceptualised by Abes, Jones and McEwens. They called their new 'advanced' model a 'Reconceptualised Model of Multiple Dimensions of Identity (R-MMDI)', utilising Kegan's (1994) ideas of meaning-making processes during identity development, and based on research on lesbian college students by Abes in 2004. In this work, (Abes, 2004) it was suggested that the inclusion of a meaning-making process in the MMDI was important because it allows the researcher to better understand the links between core and social identities as well as a relationship between contextual influences and the salience of identity dimensions. The results from Abes (2006) entail a 'meaning-making capacity served as a filter through which contextual factors are interpreted prior to influencing self-perceptions of (particular) identity and its relationship with other identity dimensions' (p. 6).

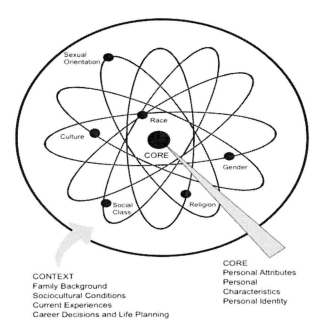

Figure 3. Model of multiple dimensions of identity (Jones and McEwen, 2000).

The re-conceptualised model (Figure 4) now consists of the following four main parts:

(i) The outer contextual influences, which are placed outside the identity circles. Illeris (2014) sees these as conditions
(ii) Social identity dimensions are now viewed in relation to personal perceptions of multiple identity dimensions. This resembles Illeris (2014) part identities
(iii) Meaning-making filter, this is placed between (i) and (ii). The filter depends on the depth and size of the mesh opening. Complex, meaning-making can be represented by increase thickness (increase depth) and smaller grid openings. Where meaning-making with less complexity is indicated as a thin filter

(lower depth) and bigger grid openings. This resembles Mezirow's (2009) dialogue element of transformational learning and Gee's (2000) discourse identity, whereas such a filter is missing in Illeris (2014) identity model (Figure 1)

(iv) Finally core indicating self-identity resembling Illeris (2014) and Robnett et al. (2015) core identity.

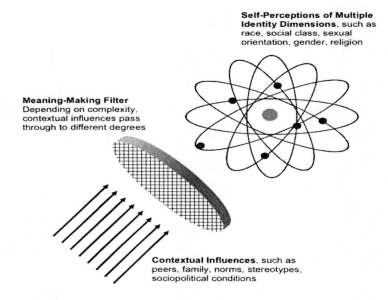

Figure 4. Reconceptualised model of multiple dimensions of identity (Abes, Jones and McEwen, 2007, p. 7).

In summary the above model (Figure 4) gives space to capture individual self-perception in the following ways:

(i) First, the meaning-making filter can allow us to capture the understanding of scientific concepts and procedures
(ii) Second, whether the meaningful positive/negative science linked influences had an impact on their self-perception of single identity or self-perception of multiple identities at the same time
(iii) Third, whether these meaningful influences have transformed one's science or non-science core

(iv) Then, the basis of the outcome could also enable to distinguish between active or passive science and/or non-science identity formation during the lifetime of the individual.

This discussion so far lead us to our own science identity model, the Sci-ID model (Salehjee, 2017). In the model (Figure 5) we envisage seven main parts:

1. ***Global forces (GF):*** These involve external influences in relation to ethnicity, gender, race, religion, class, etc., resembling Giddens's (1991) 'globalising influences'
2. ***Social agents (SA):*** As above, these are the agents that mediate the global influences with the individual through interaction and relationships. For example: parents, school, teachers, peers, churches, etc.
3. ***Transformational experiences***: These are the resultant experiences, events, triggers and interventions gained from the SA and/or GF which could have high, intermediate, low or no impact on individuals
4. ***Meaning-making filter***: We have introduced Abes et al. (2007) meaning-making filter (Figure 4), this part of the model involves an understanding of the scientific concepts. More complex meaning-making filter (a thick layer with small grid opening) allow little understanding and a less complex filter (thin layer with large grid opening) allows greater understanding of the scientific concepts being studied
5. ***Preference filter***: We have introduced this layer from Illeris's (2014) identity model (Figure 1), which constitutes Mezirow's meaning schemes (Illeris, 2014). For us these meaning schemes are the TL experiences that have been sieved by the meaning-making filter (or not). Now a preference filter will actually select the preferred (liked) experiences that have the potential of some degree to interact with individual agency. More complex filter exhibits little or no preferences and less complex filter exhibits

preferences/likes towards science. The non-preferred experiences will not proceed further inside the identity model. This filter differs from Illeris identity model (Figure 1) first, it is represented as a filter and second, it forms the second layer in our model and outermost layer in Illeris's model. As in our opinion Illeris is aware of meaning-making of the events as well as preferences however he has not separated both in his identity model

6. ***Individual Internal Agency***: This part of the model involves personal 'drive', the ways in which people can go against transformative experiences, SA and/or GF – or go with them. This layer is quite stable unless exposed to life changing (high impact) transformative experiences leading to movement (transformation) into or away from science. This layer resembles Mezirow's meaning perspectives where the higher order of pre-held schemes can be transformed based on the experiences received from the previous layer (preference layer), where critical reflection is extended further (Illeris, 2014). Illeris named this layer as personality layer, where we did not, as the intention of this review is not to look deeply into the personality theories and a huge number of personality issues but rather we are interested in self-perceptions of people towards science and non-science education and career

7. ***Core***: It resembles Abes et al. (2007) and Illeris (2014) inner most central core. Which we believe could be stable or fluid. If the transformation in IIA layer is successful or individual layer is in ambivalence then there is a possibility that the pre-held transformed viewpoints could change the core identity. We understand it in such a way that if the core is stable then transformation at the core level is quite difficult and time consuming but if the core is fluid than the transformation is relatively easier and less time consuming.

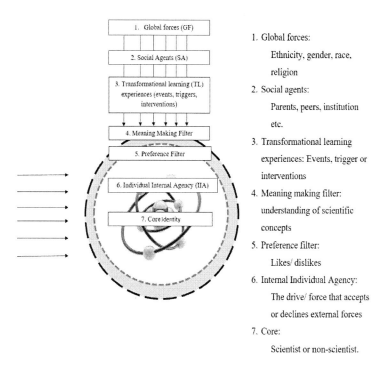

Figure 5. Sci-ID model.

We use this model to map or chart a person's real and possible life journey, the main circumstances and events that have generated – or are in the process of generating – transformation(s) in people's identity into or away from science education and career choices. We see this mapping as useful in determining both the fluid and stable nature of an individual's identity construct and, hence, signalling possible interventions. Teachers, science educators, youth workers, etc. might meet individual's needs, motivations, self-believes in either strengthening or altering the migration of individuals towards science education, science careers and, most importantly, changing negative dispositions and helping people to become scientifically literate citizens. In this next sections, we illustrate its use (Figure 6) to relate science identity model with the notions of stability and fluidity in the journey of constructing science and/or non-science identity.

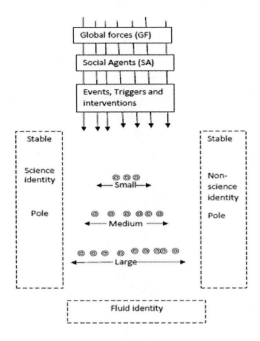

Figure 6. The migration of the people: small, medium or large movement.

We depict the model as a 'migration of people', consisting of three main regions, two extreme 'poles' and a central region. The people at the extremes can be seen to have either stable science or non-science identity. Those who populate the space between have more fluid identities. As can be seen in the science identity model (Figure 5), SA and GF could influence the movement of people towards or away from science through generating a series of external transformational learning (TL) experiences (events, triggers and interventions). These TL experiences can have a low, medium or high impact on different people. Variations in TL experience might be as follows:

(i) Large number generating a low, intermediate or high impact of TL experience (triggers, events, interventions)
(ii) Medium number generating low, intermediate or high impact of TL experiences (triggers, events, interventions)

Models of Scientific Identity 39

(iii) Small number generating a low, intermediate or high impact of TL experience (triggers, events, interventions).

These variations depend on the stability of one's identity. Therefore, (i) people can either have stable science or non-science agency, exhibiting very small or no movement away from their respective extremes, unless exposed to a large, medium or a small number of TL experiences that generates a high impact. While (ii) people with fluid IIA exhibit medium or large movement towards or away from science because, they probably have an intermediate to high impact from a large, medium or a small number of TL experiences.

(vii) Kinds of Identity Transformations

In addition to Mezirow (2000), Illeris (2014) extended transformative learning theory into progressive, regressive and restoring transformations. We will now describe our viewpoints on the three kinds of science identity transformation with examples. Our intention here is not to include Illeris (2014) collective transformation in this study, which has the potential for further research. Our brief case studies below illustrate the science identity model and the 'migration of sciencey people' to describe the three kinds of Illeris's (2014) kind of transformation.

Progressive transformative learning involves goal oriented purposeful learning with awareness of self and others. It involves progression towards the intended goal and throughout the journey making learning improved, implying actions appropriately and modifying identity accordingly to reach the desired position in life. This leads to identity change 'into something better, more proper, more promising or more rewarding', which Illeris (2014) termed progressive transformation (Illeris, 2014, p. 93). An example is as follows:

> Sam, a 40 year-old engineer, belongs to Black and Minority Ethnic (BME) community. From primary school age he believed himself to be a 'brainy person' and, reflecting on this, he sees himself to be a 'sciencey

person'. This stability in science identity coincides with the segregation that current researchers and educators have indicated in relation to ethnicity, gender, race and religion (for example Archer et al. 2013). We view, Sam's intention of being sciencey to be loosely shaped by global influences – he rejected the influence of being the only BME student in his physical engineering class and the only BME employee in his department whilst, at the same time, fulfilling his aspirations. Social agents had low impact in his 'science life' – for example, he believes that his parents were quite 'far behind' in understanding the education system, and his science teachers were less than keen in promoting science education and science careers in school. Unlike his siblings, who attended swimming lessons on every Saturday, Sam attended science club on a voluntary basis because he perceived it to be an open, independent and an un-stressful platform to fulfil his aspirations of working as an engineer.

At the time of subject selection – aged 19 – his chosen option were biology, chemistry, physics and mathematics i.e., all within the sciences. At no point did he consider opting for any non-science (humanities) subjects. Later, he decided to continue specifically with mathematics and physics, and so his meaning making filter and preference filters became increasingly focussed on these two specialisms, progressing to become a 'physical engineer'. For us, this illustrates a stable science identity and a stable belief in being a 'sciencey person'.

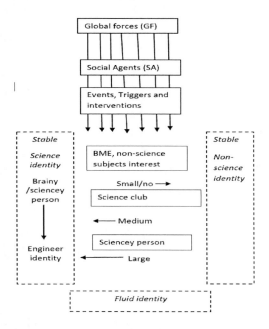

Figure 7. Charting Sam's progressive transformation.

Models of Scientific Identity   41

In summary, Sam exhibits little or no movement away from science. His identity remained securely within the domain of science and science education. His self-belief in being a 'sciencey person' made the largest impact on his developing life. Most of the movement in his choices (taking science-based school subjects, joining a science club) were impervious to larger global forces that might have taken him away from science (Figure 7).

Regressive transformations, on the other hand, involve individuals who enrol themselves in an activity or in a situation where transformation is necessary. These could be intended or situational transformations, and people might withdraw from the progressive changes despite having all the necessary challenges and support that are provided in the form of contextual influences. In this situation a progressive transformation could be experienced, say, as too demanding and unbearable despite the individual's attempts to keep up with expectations. This withdrawal leads to what Illeris terms 'regressive transformation' (Illeris, 2014). An example is as follows:

> Sarah, aged 35, is an Asian working-class woman. Her father worked in a leather factory and mother as a house wife. At the age of 15, as a part of school-based work experience, she became involved in helping local authority-assigned health professionals to improve the health conditions for children. The combination of being both an Asian working class girl (GF) aspiring to be a health professional (SA), and carrying out work experiences in helping the local community (TL), gave some meaning to her life. She eventually saw medical science as a 'dream profession'. In addition, she found one of her science teachers (SA) to be very inspirational, a teacher who always encouraged Sarah's ambition to continue with biological sciences. Moreover, one of her school's interventions was to highlight social media campaigns in bringing working class women into science education and science professions. Accordingly, Sarah's journey in constructing an identity as a medical doctor grew stronger, along with her belief that a university degree in science would provide better career opportunities, earn respect and money.
>
> At the decision-making age of 16, Sarah chose biology and English as major subjects for pre-university A-levels. English was her second choice because she loved reading and writing non-fiction stories and autobiographies. Her interest in biology as well as English exhibits a fluid

nature where, at this age, she exhibited some movement towards biology and in becoming a doctor. During A-levels, Sarah struggled to pass the biology examinations and, after retaking the exam, she passed although with less marks. This gave pause for thought, she realised she was unable to live up to her own expectations and subsequently found it too difficult to continue with medical sciences. Sarah was upset by this fairly sudden regression and therefore took up her second choice and enrolled in an English course. However, she failed again. This led Sarah to move completely out of education as well as from helping her local community, thus exhibiting a fairly regressive transformation. She began work in a local grocery shop from age 22 – where she is working to date.

Sarah's core cannot be described as stable or sufficiently forceful to make her fight against failure. Instead, a failure rooted quite deeply in her identity. This regressive TL towards education seems to have paralysed, even if opportunities/resources become available.

In summary, Sarah has exhibited movement into and away from science at different stages of her life, both movements guided by external forces and her failure in exams. She constructed a meaning for herself as 'education is not for me' resulting in regressive transformation (Figure 8).

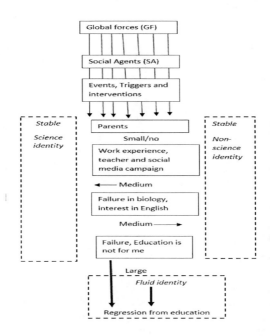

Figure 8. Charting Sarah's regressive transformation.

Models of Scientific Identity 43

Third we use 'restorative transformation' as a combination of progressive and regressive transformation. The regressive transformation above could have been sudden upsetting change but could be useful and progressive in the long run. The regression towards these adverse experiences might be useful later in life, which could act as the first step towards the initiation of progressive transformation. This type of transformation is termed by Illeris (2014) as 'restoring transformation' where we call it as reconstructive transformation because we believe progression after regression will allow a person to accept quite different TL experiences incorporated through a certain drive/or force (IIA). A theoretical example is as follows:

> Deborah aged 55, is a white middle class woman. She was expected to do a degree in chemistry, as both her parents were working in the field of chemistry and were much respected in the family and immediate community. She never felt that school science and science teachers had an influence in developing aspiration towards science. Even though, Deborah's science results were always quite impressive, she was equally good in music, arts, literature and history. At the age of 17, she found herself as sitting at cross roads, exhibiting fluid and ambivalent feelings towards science and non-science studies. She preferred chemistry over arts because of her family influences and entered chemistry undergraduate studies at university, although she later said, her 'heart was not into it'. She therefore struggled to maintain interest in chemistry classes, felt burdened and demotivated, all of which resulted in regressive transformation and movement away from the study of chemistry. While discussing this with her personal tutor, she realised that chemistry was simply 'not for her'. After a thoughtful journey, Deborah realized that her real interest lay in creative and imaginative arts. At the age of 20, her movement towards studying arts grew stronger and her identity constructs develop towards stability in arts. This resulted in a progressive transformation in accordance with her sense of individual agency. Currently, she is a university lecturer in modern arts.

In summary, Deborah exhibited movement into and away from science at different stages of her life. At the initial stages she exhibited fluid nature – where parental and community influences guided her choice of chemistry. Later, feeling detached from chemistry, she identified herself as 'an arty person' resulting in progression into arts after a regression from chemistry (Figure 9).

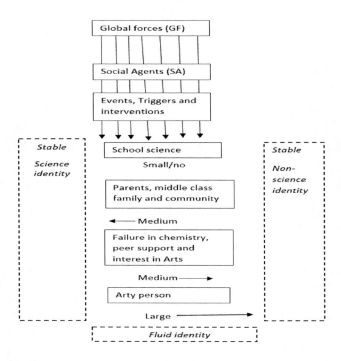

Figure 9. Charting Deborah's reconstructive transformation.

Similar to the above examples of Sam, Sarah and Deborah, Salehjee (2017) has tested the models to chart science lives of twelve science and non-science professionals (Salehjee & Watts, 2015), 123 university students and thirty girls. For future research, we are determined to map science lives of people from different stages of their lives and help to device specific interventions to avoid regression and movement away from science.

CONCLUSION

In this chapter we have reviewed and analysed the aspects of global forces (GF), social agents (SA), Transformative learning (TL) experiences, Individual Internal Agency (IIA) and their incorporation in a few key science identity research models. We also discussed the transformation of

Models of Scientific Identity

identities using identity models and kinds of transformation. Moreover, researchers in the area of science education also need to promote public understanding of science and evaluate ways that stop students 'closing science doors' too early in their lives. We recommend that researchers use the Sci-ID model and adapt it to explore the duality of external forces and agency in individuals from schools, colleges, universities, science and non-science-based professional workplaces, etc.

From our discussions of identity and identity transformations, it is quite clear to us that there in a gap in promoting lifelong learning in science. As school pupils pass the age of compulsory education, and later gain science or non-science based careers, their identities become quite stable either towards science or to non-science. Some are anti-science, some pro-science and we can identify them as 'sciencey' or 'non-sciencey' people. Moreover, to cater for this, various intervention strategies have been employed in the UK – for example, the ASPIREs project. However, we believe that schools ignore or neglect the vast majority – the young people who are fluid in their aspirations. In our view, schools and teachers need to find simple ways of implementing 'science interventions' to cater for students with both stable pro-science and those with fluid identities. There is a clear need for well researched and evaluated strategies/ interventions to encourage fluidity in non-science students, and work towards incorporating stability among those fluid students. They need to consider the meaning-making of science content along with the preferences, enjoyment and the fun element of laboratory work, out of school visits, etc. Therefore, we strongly encourage science teachers to carryout action research involving not only designing and implementing interventions but also evaluating and modifying their plans. They need to identify stable and fluid people, which requires effort in talking to people or communities – understanding their stories, life journey, finding out what are the things that move them away or towards science and design simple interventions accordingly for the schools and teachers (Watts, 2015, 2018).

For example, John is 38 years old and does not have a university degree, works in a local shop, hated science in school. However, he follows Tim Peake's journey to the International Space Station and is fascinated by space and rockets. In this respect, his fascination is similar to Sam's case above. However, he did not have the same opportunities as Sam, and his fascination could not translate into a force that would allow him to become a scientist. Even though he is not in the field of science his fascination is well and alive, and the question is: What can be done to foster and support this interest? Like Falk (2005), we see the promotion of mechanisms and funding as essential to enabling lifelong learning in local communities, churches, mosques, libraries, museums, community centers, science fairs in local parks, and so on. This strategy would raise public awareness could encourage local people to gain more scientific knowledge in their field of interest, perhaps even encourage more towards gaining qualifications. Moreover, it stands to encourage people to actually re-consider and challenge any anti-science predispositions that 'science is not for them'. That is, we need to find ways to help people to 'light their motivational fuse' into sciences by talking to people about their 'science lives, school choices and natural tendencies' (Salehjee & Watts, 2015).

REFERENCES

Abes, E. S., Jones, S. R. & McEwen, M. K. (2007). Reconceptualizing the model of multiple dimensions of identity: The role of meaning-making capacity in the construction of multiple identities. *Journal of college student development.*, *48*(1), pp. 1-22.

Abes, E. S. & Jones, S. R. (2004). Meaning-making capacity and the dynamics of lesbian college students' multiple dimensions of identity. *Journal of college student development.*, *45*(6), pp. 612-632.

Albright, J., Towndrow, P. A., Kwek, D. & Tan, A. L. (2008). Identity and agency in science education: reflections from the far side of the world. *Cultural Studies of Science Education*, *3*(1), pp. 145-156.

Archer, L. & DeWitt, J. (2016). *Understanding Young People's Science Aspirations: How students form ideas about 'becoming a scientist'.* New York, N: Routledge.

Archer, L., Dawson, E., Seakins, A., DeWitt, J., Godec, S. & Whitby, C. (2016). "I'm Being a Man Here": Urban Boys' Performances of Masculinity and Engagement With Science During a Science Museum Visit. *Journal of the Learning Sciences*, (just-accepted).

Archer, L. & DeWitt, J. (2015). Science aspirations and gender identity: Lessons from the ASPIRES project. In Henriksen, E.K., Dillon, J. and Ryder, J. eds. *Understanding student participation and choice in science and technology education.* Dordrecht: Springer, pp. 89-102.

Archer, L., Dewitt, J. & Osborne, J. (2015[a]). Is science for us? black students' and parents' views of science and science careers. *Science education.*, *99* (2), pp. 199-237.

Archer, L., Dawson, E., DeWitt, J., Seakins, A. & Wong, B. (2015[b]). Science capital: A conceptual, methodological, and empirical argument for extending bourdieusian notions of capital beyond the arts. *Journal of Research in Science Teaching*, *52*(7), pp. 922-948.

Archer, L., DeWitt, J. & Willis, B. (2014[a]). Adolescent boys' science aspirations: Masculinity, capital, and power. *Journal of Research in Science Teaching*, *51*(1), pp. 1-30.

Archer, L., DeWitt, J., Osborne, J., Dillon, J., Willis, B. & Wong, B. (2014[b]). *ASPIRES. Young people's science and career aspirations, age*, 10 –14. London: Kings College.

Archer, L., DeWitt, J., Osborne, J., Dillon, J., Willis, B. & Wong, B. (2010). "Doing" science versus "being" a scientist: Examining 10/11-year-old schoolchildren's constructions of science through the lens of identity. *Science Education*, *94*(4), pp. 617–639.

Archer, L., DeWitt, J., Osborne, J., Dillon, J., Willis, B. & Wong, B. (2012). Science Aspirations, Capital, and Family Habitus: How Families Shape Children's Engagement and Identification with Science. *American Educational Research Journal*, *49*(5), pp. 881-908.

Archer, L., DeWitt, J., Osborne, J., Dillon, J., Willis, B. & Wong, B. (2013). Not Girly, not sexy, not glamorous: Primary school girls' and parents' constructions of science aspirations. *Pedagogy, Culture & Society.*, *21* (1), pp. 171-194.

Beauchamp, G. & Parkinson, J. (2008). Pupils' attitudes towards school science as they transfer from an ICT-rich primary school to a secondary school with fewer ICT resources: Does ICT matter? *Education and Information Technologies*, *13*(2), pp. 103-118.

Block, D. (2013). The structure and agency dilemma in identity and intercultural communication research. *Language and Intercultural Communication*, *13* (2), pp. 126-147.

Bourdieu, P. & Passeron, J. C. (1990). *Reproduction in education, society and culture*. 2nd edition. London: Sage.

Bourdieu, P. (1990) *In other words: Essay towards a reflexive sociology*. Cambridge: Polity.

Bourdieu, P. (1986). The forms of capital. In J. C. Richardson. ed. *Handbook of theory and research for the sociology of education*. New York: Greenwood Press, pp. 241-258.

Bourdieu, Pierre. (1986). The Forms of Capital. In John Richardson, Ed. *Handbook of Theory and Research for the Sociology of Education*. New York: Greenwood Press, pp. 241-258.

Bourdieu, P. & Passeron, J. C. (1977). *Reproduction in education, society and culture*. Beverly Hills: Sage.

Brickhouse, N. W. & Potter, J. T. (2001). Young women's scientific identity formation in an urban context. *Journal of research in science teaching*, *38* (8), pp. 965-980.

Brickhouse, N. W., Lowery, P. & Schultz, K. (2000). What kind of a girl does science? The construction of school science identities. *Journal of research in science teaching*, *37*(5), pp. 441-458.

Burke, P. J. & Stets, J. E. (2009). *Identity theory*. New York NY: Oxford University Press.

Carambo, C. (2015). Social, Cultural and Emotional Contexts of Transformative Learning Environments. In Milne, C., Tobin, K. and DeGennaro, D. eds. *Sociocultural Studies and Implications for Science Education*. Netherlands: Springer, pp. 155-180.

Carlone, H. B., & Johnson, A. (2007). Understanding the science experiences of successful women of color: Science identity as an analytic lens. *Journal of Research in Science Teaching*, *44*(8), pp. 1187–1218.

Chapman, A. & Feldman, A. (2016). Cultivation of science identity through authentic science in an urban high school classroom. *Cultural Studies of Science Education*, pp. 1-23.

Claussen, S. & Osborne, J. (2012) Bourdieu's notion of cultural capital and its implications for science curriculum. *Science Education*, *97*(1), pp. 58-79.

Darragh, L. (2016). Identity research in mathematics education, *Education Studies in Mathematics*, *93*, 19–33. DOI 10.1007/s10649-016-9696-5.

D'Amato, L. G. & Krasny, M. E. (2011). Outdoor adventure education: Applying transformative learning theory to understanding instrumental learning and personal growth in environmental education. *Journal of Environmental Education*, *42*(4), pp. 237–254.

DiMaggio, P. (1982). Cultural capital and school success: The impact of status culture participation on the grades of US high school students. *American sociological review*, *47*(2), pp. 189-201.

Dweck, C. S. (1999). *Self-theories: Their role in motivation, personality and development*. Philadelphia: Psychology Press.

Dweck, C. (2008). *Mindsets and math/science achievement*. New York, NY: Carnegie Corporation of New York, Institute for Advanced Study, Commission on Mathematics and Science Education.

Elmesky, R. & Seiler, G. (2007). Movement expressiveness, solidarity and the (re) shaping of African American students' scientific identities. *Cultural Studies of Science Education*, *2*(1), pp. 73-103.

Erikson, E. H. (1982). *The lifecycle completed*. New York, USA: Norton.

Erel, U. (2010). Migrating cultural capital: Bourdieu in migration studies. *Sociology*, *44*(4), pp. 642-660.

Erikson, E. (1973). Eight ages of man. In Bowman, C.C., 1973. *Humanistic sociology; readings*. McGraw-Hill Primis Custom Publishing, p. 68 -82.

Erikson, E. H. (1968). *Identity: Youth and crisis*. New York: Norton.

Estrada, M., Woodcock, A., Hernandez, P. R. & Schultz, P. W. (2010). Toward a model of social influence that explains minority student integration into the scientific community. *Journal of Educational Psychology*, [Accessed 09/10/14]. 103(1), pp. 206–222. doi: 10.1037/a0020743.

Falk, J. H. (2005). Free-choice environmental learning: framing the discussion. *Environmental education research*, *11*(3), 265-280.

Gee, J. P. (2000). Identity as an analytic lens for research in education. *Review of research in education*, *25*, pp. 99-125. [Online] [Accessed 09/10/17]. Available from: http://rre.sagepub.com/content/25/1/99.full.pdf+html.

Giddens, A. (1991). *Modernity and self-identity: Self and society in the late modern age*. Stanford: Stanford University Press.

Gilmartin, S. K., Li, E. & Aschbacher, P. (2006). The relationship between interest in physical science/engineering, science class experiences, and family contexts: Variations by gender and race/ethnicity among secondary students. *Journal of Women and Minorities in Science and Engineering*, *12*(2-3). [Online] [Accessed 20/11/2014]. Available from:10.1615/JWomenMinorScienEng.v12.i2-3.50.

Hampden-Thompson, G. & Bennett, J. (2013). Science Teaching and Learning Activities and Students' Engagement in Science. *International Journal of Science Education*, *35*(8), 1325-1343.

Hassard, J. & Dias, M. (2009). *The Art of Teaching Science: Enquiry and innovation in middle school and high school.* 2nd Ed. New York and London: Routledge.

Hattam, R. & Zipin, L. (2009). Towards pedagogical justice. *Discourse: Studies in the cultural Politics of Education*, *30*(3), pp. 297-301.

Hazari, Z., Cass, C. & Beattie, C. (2015). Obscuring power structures in the physics classroom: Linking teacher positioning, student engagement, and physics identity development. *Journal of Research in Science Teaching*, *52*(6), pp. 735-762.

Hazari, Z., Potvin, G., Lock, R. M., Lung, F., Sonnert, G. & Sadler, P. M. (2013). Factors that affect the physical science career interest of female students: Testing five common hypotheses. *Physical Review Special Topics-Physics Education Research*, *9*(2), pp. 020115.

Hazari, Z., Sonnert, G., Sadler, P. M. & Shanahan, M. C. (2010). Connecting high school physics experiences, outcome expectations, physics identity, and physics career choice: A gender study. *Journal of Research in Science Teaching, 47*(8), pp. 978-1003.

Heddy, B. & Pugh, K. (2015). Bigger is not always better: Should educators aim for big transformative learning events or small transformative experiences? *Journal of Transformative Learning, 3*(1), pp. 52-58.

House of Commons Children, Schools and Families Committee. (2010). *Training of Teachers: Fourth report of session 2009 – 10*, Volume *2* [Online]. [Accessed 20 July 2010]. Available from: http://books. google.com/books?id=c7aIl38yPtUC&pg=PA178&dq=ofsted+continu ing+professional+development+for+teachers+in+schools&hl=en&ei=z vVSTPCNKJSI4gbS9fTgAw&sa=X&oi=book_result&ct=result&resn um=4&ved=0CEIQ6AEwAw#v=onepage&q=ofsted%20continuing%2 0professio.

Hulleman, C. S. & Cordray, D. S. (2009). Moving from the lab to the field: The role of fidelity and achieved relative Intervention strength. *Journal of Research on Educational Effectiveness, 2*(1), pp. 88–110.

Hyde, J. S., Canning, E. A., Rozek, C. S., Clarke, E., Hulleman, C. S. & Harackiewicz, J. M. (2016). The Role of Mothers' Communication in Promoting Motivation for Math and Science Course-Taking in High School. *Journal of Research on Adolescence*. [Online]. [Accessed 12/12/2016]. Available from: doi:10.1111/jora.12253.

Illeris, K. (2014). *Transformative learning and identity*. London and New York: Routledge.

Ing, M. (2014). Gender differences in the influence of early perceived parental support on student mathematics and science achievement and STEM career attainment. *International Journal of Science and Mathematics Education, 12*(5), pp. 1221-1239.

Jackson, P. W. (1986). *The practice of teaching*. New York: Teachers College Press.

Jarvis, P. (2013) Learning to be a person East and West. *Comparative Education*. [Online], *49*(1), pp. 4-15. [Accessed 20/10/15]. Available from: doi: 10.1080/03050068.2012.740216.

Jarvis, P. (2009). *Learning to be a person in society*. London and New York: Routledge.

Jenkins, R. B. (1992). *Pierre Bourdieu*. London: Routledge.

Jensen, E. & Wright, D. (2015). Critical Response to Archer et al. (2015). "Science Capital": A Conceptual, Methodological, and Empirical Argument for Extending Bourdieusian Notions of Capital Beyond the Art. *Science Education*, *99* (6), pp. 1143-1146.

Jeynes, W. H. (2010). Parental involvement and encouraging that involvement: Implications for school-based programs. *Teachers College Record*, *112*(3), pp. 747–774.

Jones, S. R. & McEwen, M. K. (2000). A conceptual model of multiple dimensions of identity. *Journal of college student development.*, *41*(4), pp. 405-414.

Jungert, T. & Koestner, R. (2015). Science adjustment, parental and teacher autonomy support and the cognitive orientation of science students. *Educational Psychology*, *35*(3), pp. 361-376.

Kane, J. M. (2012). Young African American children constructing academic and disciplinary identities in an urban science classroom. *Science Education*, *96*(3), pp. 457-487.

Kegan, R. (2009). What "form" transforms; A constructive developmental approach to transformative learning. In Illeris, K. ed. *Contemporary theories of learning: learning theorists... in their own words*. London and New York: Routledge, p. 35-52.

Kegan, R. (1994). *In Over Our Heads: The Mental Complexity of Modern Life*. Cambridge MA: Harvard University Press.

Kelman, H. C. (2006). Interests, relationships, identities: Three central issues for individuals and groups in negotiating their social environment. *Annu. Rev. Psychol.*, *57*, pp. 1-26.

King, A. (2000). Thinking with Bourdieu against Bourdieu: A 'Practical' Critique of the Habitus. *Sociological Theory*, *18*(3), pp. 417-433.

Lave, J. & Wenger, E. (1991). *Situated learning: Legitimate peripheral participation*. Cambridge, UK: Cambridge University Press.

Lee, Y. J. (2012). Identity-based research in science education. In B. Fraser, K. Tobin, & C. McRobbie. eds. *Second international handbook of science education*. Dordrecht: Springer, pp. 35–45.

Lerman, S. (2001). Cultural, discursive psychology: A sociocultural approach to studying the teaching and learning of mathematics. *Educational Studies in Mathematics*, *46*(1/3), 87–113. doi:10.2307/3483241.

Lock, R. M., Hazari, Z. & Potvin, G. (2013). Physics career intentions: The effect of physics identity, math identity, and gender. In *2012 Physics education research conference.*, *1513*(1), pp. 262-265. AIP Publishing.

Loehle, C. (2010). *Becoming a successful scientist. Strategic thinking for scientific discovery*. Cambridge: Cambridge University Press.

MacDonald, A. (2014). "Not for people like me?" Under-represented groups in science, technology and engineering. A summary of the evidence: the facts, the fiction and what we should do next. *Women in science, technology and engineering* (WI S E). [Online]. [Accesed 10/10/16]. Available from: http:// www.equalityanddiversity.net/ docs/ not_for_people_like_me.pdf.

Mandler, D., Mamlok-Naaman, R., Blonder, R., Yayon, M. & Hofstein, A. (2012). High-school chemistry teaching through environmentally oriented curricula. *Chemistry Education Research and Practice*, *13*(2), pp. 80–92.

Mezirow, J. (2009). Transformtive learning theory. In Mezirow, J., Taylor, W. and associates. *Transformative learning in practice: Insights from community, workplace, and higher education*. San Francisco, CA:Josey-Bass.

Mezirow, J. (2000). Learning to think like an adult. In J. Mezirow (Ed.), Learning as transformation: Critical perspectives on a theory in progress. San Francisco, CA: Jossey Bass.Midgley, M. (2013). *Science and poetry*. Routledge, pp. 3–34.

Mezirow, J. (1996). Transformation theory of adult learning. In M. R.Welton. ed. *In defence of the lifeworld*. New York: SUNY Press, pp. 39–70.

Mezirow, J. (1991). *Transformative dimensions of adult learning*. Jossey-Bass, 350 Sansome Street, San Francisco, CA 94104-1310.

Mezirow, J. (1990). How critical reflection triggers transformative learning. *Fostering critical reflection in adulthood.*, *1*, p. 20. [Online]. [Accessed 10/10/17]. Available from: http:// s3.amazonaws.com/ academia.edu.documents/30281715/critical-reflection.pdf?AWS AccessKeyId=AKIAJ56TQJRTWSMTNPEA&Expires=1484429283& Signature=PZ7Ofi3jCBXeU2IZJKauMsuWKxc%3D&response-content-disposition=inline%3B%20filename%3DHow_critical_reflection_triggers_transfo.pdf.

Mezirow, J. & Marsick, V. (1978). *Education for perspective transformation: Women's re-entry programs in community colleges.* New York: Center for Adult Education, Teachers College, Columbia University.

Nohl, A. M. (2015). Typical Phases of Transformative Learning: A Practice-Based Model. *Adult Education Quarterly*, *65* (1), pp. 35-49.

Nunes, T., Bryant, P., Strand, S., Hillier, J., Barros, R. & Miller-Firedmann, J. (2017). *Review of SES and Science Learning in Formal Educational Settings*. A Report Prepared for the Education Endowment Foundation and the Royal Society. Oxford, University of Oxford.

Osborne, J. (2014). Teaching scientific practices: Meeting the challenge of change. *Journal of Science Teacher Education*, *25*(2), pp. 177-196.

Pike, A. G. & Dunne, M. (2011). Student reflections on choosing to study science post-16. [Online]. *Cultural Studies of Science Education*, *6*, 485–500. Available from: doi:10.1007/s11422-010-9273-7.

Reid, A. & McCallum, F. (2014). 'Becoming your best': student perspectives on community in the pursuit of aspirations. *The Australian Educational Researcher*, *41*(2), pp. 195-207.

Rodogno, R. (2012). Personal Identity Online. *Philosophy and Technology.*, *25*(3), pp. 309–328.

Robnett, R. D., Chemers, M. M. & Zurbriggen, E. L. (2015). Longitudinal associations among undergraduates' research experience, self-efficacy, and identity. *Journal of Research in Science Teaching, 52*(6), pp. 847-867.

Rodogno, R. (2012). Personal Identity Online. *Philosophy and Technology., 25*(3), pp. 309–328.

Rodrigues, S. (2014). Language and communication in the science classroom. In D.M. Watts.ed. *Debates in Science Education*, London: Routledge.

Ransome, P. (2010). *Social theory for beginners*. UK: Policy Press.

Reay, D., Crozier, G. & Clayton, J. (2010). "Fitting in" or "standing out": Workingclass students in UK higher education. *British Educational Research Journal, 36*(1), 107–124.

Reay, D. (2004). Education and Cultural capital: The implications of changing trends in education policies. *Cultural Trends, 13*(2), pp. 73-86.

Roth, W. & Middleton, D. (2006). Knowing what you tell, telling what you know: Uncertainty and asymmetries of meaning in interpreting graphical data. *Cultural Studies of Science Education, 1* (1), pp. 11–81.

Salehjee, S. (2017). *Making scientists: Developing a model of science identity*. Un-published PhD thesis.

Salehjee, S., Ludhra, G. & Watts, D. M. (2018). (in press) Young South-Asian women and science identity. *Cultural Studies of Science Education.*

Salehjee, S. & Watts, D. M. (2015). Science lives: school choices and 'natural tendencies'. *International Journal of Science Education, 37*(4), pp. 727-743.

Seginer, R. (2006). Parents' educational involvement: A developmental ecological perspective. *Parenting: Science and Practice, 6* (1), pp. 1–48.

Spillane, M. (2000). *Branding yourself: How to look, sound and behave your way to success.* Pan: London: Sidgwick & Jackson.

Stuckey, M., Hofstein, A., Mamlok-Naaman, R. & Eilks, I. (2013). The meaning of 'relevance' in science education and its implications for the science curriculum. *Studies in Science Education, 49*(1), pp. 1-34.

Stinson, D. & Bullock, E. (2012). Critical postmodern theory in mathematics education research: A praxis of uncertainty. *Educational Studies in Mathematics, 80*, 41–55. doi:10.1007/s10649-012-9386-x.

Sullivan, A. (2002). Bourdieu and Education: How Useful is Bourdieu's Theory for Researchers? *The Netherlands Journal of Social Sciences, 38*(2), pp. 144- 166.

Tao, V. Y. (2016). Understanding Chinese Students' Achievement Patterns: Perspectives from Social-Oriented Achievement Motivation. In *The Psychology of Asian Learners.* Springer Singapore, (pp. 621-634).

Taylor, C. (2009). *A Good School for Every Child: How to Improve Our Schools.* UK: Routledge. [Online]. [Accessed 10/09/16]. Available from:http://books.google.com/books?id=6ZWRgVl454MC&pg=PA73 &dq=science+specialist+teachers&hl=en&ei=rYtSTOCTDIfb4Ab5jN 3_Ag&sa=X&oi=book_result&ct=result&resnum=5&ved=0CEMQ6A EwBA#v=onepage&q=walter&f=false.

Tissenbaum, M., Lui, M. & Slotta, J. D. (2012). Co-Designing Collaborative Smart Classroom Curriculum for Secondary School Science. *J. UCS., 18*(3), pp. 327-352.

Wang, M. T., Eccles, J. S. & Kenny, S. (2013). Not lack of ability but more choice individual and gender differences in choice of careers in science, technology, engineering, and mathematics. *Psychological Science, 24*(5), pp. 770-775.

Wood, R. & Ashfield, J. (2008). The use of the interactive whiteboard for creative teaching and learning in literacy and mathematics: a case study. *British journal of educational technology, 39*(1), pp. 84-96.

Welton, M. R. (1995). *In defence of the lifeworld, critical perspectives on adult learning.* Albany, NY: SUNY Press.

Yeager, D. S. & Walton, G. M. (2011). Social-psychological interventions in education They're not magic. *Review of educational Research, 81*(2), pp. 267-301.

BIOGRAPHICAL SKETCH

Dr. Saima Salehjee, PhD

Affiliation: University of Strathclyde

Education: PhD in Science Education

Business Address: University of Strathclyde, The School of Education Lord Hope Building, 141 St James Road, Glasgow, G4 0LT

Research and Professional Experience: Saima's research focuses on science identity and identity transformations over a lifespan of individuals from a different ethnic, religious and sexual backgrounds. Saima is a passionate science lecturer, motivating her student teachers to implement science interventions in schools and to research the impact of these interventions. Her aim is to inspire more primary and secondary school students to progress into STEM education and careers as future scientists.

Professional Appointments: Saima Salehjee is a Chemistry Lecturer in the Department of Education, Strathclyde University, Glasgow, responsible for teaching and research work with particular emphasis on STEM education.

Honors: She was nominated for the Brunel Doctoral Research Prize in 2017 and received the Grace Peeling Memorial Prize for her MA in Educational Management in 2011. She is an Associate Fellow of the Higher Education Academy (AFHEA), Associate Member of Royal Society of Chemistry (AMRSC) and RSC treasurer.

Publications from the Last 3 Years:

Watts, M., Salehjee, S., Essex, J., But is it science? *Early Childhood Development and Care,* Vol 187, pp. 274-283, (2017). http://dx.doi.org/10.1080/03004430.2016.1237566

Salehjee, S., The impact of science interventions: to enhance science teaching and learning in a secondary school, in *International Academic Conference on Teaching, Learning and E-learning* in Budapest, Hungary, July 2016 (2016).

Salehjee S., Being sciencey: science identity, inherent inclination and social influence, *47th Australasian Science Education Research Association annual conference* (2016).

Salehjee, S., The impact of science interventions for secondary school girls, *Brunel University London Equality and Diversity Conference* (2016).

Salehjee, S., Watts, M., Science lives: school choices and 'natural tendencies', *International Journal of Science Education* Vol 37, pp. 727-743, (2015); http://dx.doi.org/10.1080/09500693.2015.1013075.

Professor Mike Watts

Affiliation: Brunel University, London

Education: After qualifying as a teacher at Doncaster College of Education he taught physics and science in Hackney, London and Kingston, Jamaica before entering educational research at University of Surrey, where he led a project investigating young people's understanding of physics. He left Surrey having established a successful project and completed his doctorate, to join the Schools Council's Secondary Science Curriculum Review as Project Officer. In 1986 Mike joined Roehampton University as lecturer and, in the following years moved to Senior Lecturer, Reader, Professor, Dean of School, Federal Professor and then Principal of Froebel College.

Business Address: Brunel University London. College of Business, Arts and Social Sciences, Department of Education, Halsbury Building, Brunel University London, Uxbridge, UB8 3PH, United Kingdom

Research and Professional Experience: I have carried out major studies of classroom interactions often, but not always, concerning the learning of science. My recent work has looked at the means by which learner's own questions can be used as a basis for inquiry-based teaching, the manner in which feelings and emotions shape learning, and modes in which classroom technologies can be used to enhance learning processes. In 2003 I was awarded a Higher Education Academy National Teaching Fellowship for his excellence in teaching, and have used the award to further research and scholarship into teaching and learning in higher education. In 2004 I was elected a Fellow of the Institute of Physics. I have undertaken consultancy work for universities in Brazil, been part of a World Bank Rapid Response team within Latin America, and a review team for teacher education in Lithuania. I am currently a consultant to the Teaching Council of Ireland and external examiner for the National University of Ireland.

Professional Appointments: Honors: In 2003 he was awarded a Higher Education Academy National Teaching Fellowship for his excellence in teaching, and has used the award to further research and scholarship into teaching and learning in higher education. In 2004 he was elected a Fellow of the Institute of Physics. He is an honorary visiting Professor at Dublin City University, and University of Aveiro in Portugal, and an external examiner for University College Cork.

I have been a consultant for the Teaching Council of Ireland and external examiner for the National University of Ireland. I am currently working with Institute of Education at the University of Mauritius.

Publications from the Last 3 Years:
Ramma, Y., Bholoa, A., Watts, M., Nadal, P. S., (2017) Teaching and learning physics using technology: Making a case for the affective domain, *Education Inquiry*, 1-27.

Kanhadilok, P., Watts, M. (2017). Youth at play: some observations from a science museum. *International Journal of Adolescence and Youth* 22 (2), 179-194.

Silby, A. Watts M., (2017). Early years science education: a contemporary look *Early Child Development and Care* 187 (2), 179-180.

Watts, M., Salehjee, S., Essex J. (2017). But is it science? *Early child development and care* 187 (2), 274-283.

Ramma, Y., Bholoa, A., Watts, D. M., Samy, M., (2017). *A paradigm shift in the teaching and learning of science using technology in Mauritius: Making a case for incorporating the affective domain.* Taylor & Francis Open.

da Silva Lopes, B., Pedrosa-de-Jesus, H., Watts, M., (2016). The Old Questions Are the Best: Striving against Invalidity in Qualitative Research. *Theory and Method in Higher Education Research*, 1-22.

Crowe, N. Watts, M. (2016). We're just like Gok, but in reverse: Ana Girls–empowerment and resistance in digital communities. *International Journal of Adolescence and Youth* 21 (3), 379-390

Pedrosa-de-Jesus, H., Leite, S., Watts, M., (2016). *'Question Moments': A Rolling Programme of Question Opportunities in Classroom Science Research in Science Education* 46 (3), 329-341

Watts, D. M., Da Silva Lopes, B. M., Pedrosa de Jesus, H., (2016). *The old questions are the best: striving against invalidity in qualitative research.*

Kanhadilok, P., Zwozdiak-Myers, P. Watts, D. (2016). *Western science and indigenous wisdom: Toys at the touch point.* Springer Verlag (Germany).

Crowe, N. Watts, M., (2016). Geographies of Trolls, Grief Tourists, and Playing with Digital Transgression. *Play and Recreation, Health and Wellbeing*, 387-404.

Zwozdiak-Myers, P. D., Watts, M., Kanhadilok P., (2016). *Family science and intergenerational learning.*

Malthouse, R., Watts, M., Roffey-Barentsen J., (2015). Reflective questions, self-questioning and managing professionally situated practice. *Research in Education* 94 (1), 71-87.

Watts, M., (2015). Public understanding of plant biology: Voices from the bottom of the garden. *International Journal of Science Education*, Part B 5 (4), 339-356.

Silby, A., Watts M., (2015). Making the tacit explicit: children's strategies for classroom writing. *British Educational Research Journal* 41 (5), 801-819.

Salehjee, S., Watts M., (2015). Science lives: School choices and 'natural tendencies'. *International Journal of Science Education* 37 (4), 727-743.

Crowe, N., Watts M., (2015). Geographies of Trolls, Grief Tourists, and Playing with Digital Transgression. *Play, recreation, health and well-being*, 1-18.

Watts, D. M., Pedrosa-de-Jesus, H., Moreira, A., da Silva Lopes, B., Guerra, C. (2015). *A study of academic development in universities through innovative approaches in teaching, assessment and feedback.*

Watts, D. M., Pedrosa-de-Jesus, H., Moreira, A., da Silva Lopes, B., Guerra, C., (2015). *Academic growth and scholarship of teaching and learning: The impact of research.*

Thaufeega, F., Crowe, N., Watts D. M., (2015). *Institute and learner readiness for e-learning in the Maldives.* IATED.

In: Science and Technology Education ISBN: 978-1-53613-717-0
Editor: Steffen Pabst © 2018 Nova Science Publishers, Inc.

Chapter 2

STRATEGY VERSUS REALITY IN TECHNOLOGY EDUCATION AT BASIC SCHOOLS IN SLOVAKIA

Alena Hašková[1], PhD and Silvia Manduľáková[2], PhD*
[1]Faculty of Education,
Constantine the Philosopher University, Nitra, Slovakia
[2]Eductech, Vranov nad Topľou, Slovakia

ABSTRACT

Technology has always constituted an important facet of culture. The progress of technology has influenced – even determined – the development of every type of society. This is why technology education represents, or at least should represent, an essential component of general education. This chapter presents on the one hand a synthesis report on the development strategies of technology education carried out at basic schools in Slovakia (lower secondary education – ISCED 2) and on the other hand the results of survey research aimed at revealing the practical reality of technology teaching at these schools (the approaches of students, teachers and school leaders to technology education; the status

---

* Corresponding Author Email: ahaskova@ukf.sk.

of subjects within technology education and their curricula; the creation of appropriate conditions for teaching technology education etc.).

The education policy of the European Union calls for the support of school development and the modernization and improvement in quality of education. In accordance with the policy of the EU, in their *Reports on the State of the Education System and Systematic Steps for its Development* successive Slovak governments have announced a national education policy and within that significant attention has also been paid to technology education at all levels of education. In the synthesis report, government announcements aimed at the support of technology education and steps adopted by government are analyzed, and the relevant benefits and costs are evaluated. Ultimately, despite some differences in the government announcements, each of them declares support for further development of vocational education and increasing students' interest in it (in accordance with labor market needs).

To discover the reality, i.e., to find out how education policy statements related to technology education and related legislation are reflected in practice, and to find out their impact on teaching practice at the lower level of secondary education, survey research was carried out. The research was based on semi-structured personal interviews with technology teachers working at basic schools, via a research sample in which all regions of Slovakia were represented. As the research results show, despite the proclaimed good intentions of the different strategies, programs and reforms, the reality is different – the most worrying finding is that the status of the subject of technology (by means of which technology education at basic schools is carried out) is on the decline. So the questions are: What are the reasons for this state of affairs? What should be done about it? What are the challenges for schools/decision makers resulting from this state of affairs?

1. TECHNOLOGY EDUCATION OF CHILDREN AND YOUTH

Technology has always constituted an important facet of culture. The progress of technology has influenced – even determined – the development of every type of society. Application of technological knowledge in practice represents a precondition for the prosperity of a society, and not only recent societies but also future ones. The principal initiators of any application of technological knowledge, innovation or change have always been, and for the foreseeable future will remain, human beings. This is why, apart from creative, educated people in general, each society also needs creative, educated technicians and engineers. And this is why technology education has always been an integral part of school education, although in different types of societies and different countries this kind of education has been carried out in different ways. In some countries we can find it incorporated within the scope of the taught science subjects while in others we can find this education incorporated within the school curriculum as an independent school subject under different names.

The importance of technology education has been repeatedly stressed by UNESCO at sessions of its general conference as well as in its official documents and education strategies. Serving as an example of this fact is an extract from the UNESCO document *Recommendation Concerning Technical and Vocational Education*, adopted by the General Conference of 1962 and revised in 1974 (UNESCO, 1974):

> *An initiation to technology and to the world of work should be an essential component of general education without which this education is incomplete. An understanding of the technological facet of modern culture in both its positive and negative attributes, and an appreciation of work requiring practical skills should thereby be acquired. This initiation should further be a major concern in educational reform and change with a view to greater democratization of education. It should be a required element in the curriculum, beginning in primary education and continuing through the early years of secondary education.*

The content of technology education should comprise the study of various types of techniques and technologies with a stress on the acquisition of practical skills, attitudes, understanding and knowledge relating to occupations in various sectors of commercial, economic and social life. Following the UNESCO proclamation, technology education should be understood primarily as an integral part of education, secondly as a means of preparing for employment, and last but not least as an aspect of continuing education.

Technology education at school gives students the opportunity to make sense of theoretical knowledge they have acquired and to recognize the coherence between the theoretical subjects taught at school and the technical products surrounding them in their everyday lives. Technology education represents a field with a close interconnection with history, physics, biology, mathematics and many other disciplines. It gives students the opportunity to familiarize themselves with different occupational fields and to acquire broad knowledge and basic skills applicable in a number of occupations. The importance of technology education in evoking and influencing young people's interest in their prospective professional career is a reason to incorporate technology education into compulsory education as early as possible.

The society we live in currently is indisputably technology-based. In the context of a technology-based society one would logically expect science and technology education to be obligatory at primary and secondary schools, and students to be interested in continuing their career education in various technical study branches. But the contrary is true. For a long time the branches of science and technical or engineering study have been less favored disciplines and students have not been very interested in studying them (Lamanauskas, Gedrovics, Raipulis, 2004; Hus, Aberšek, 2007; Dopita, Grecmanová, 2008; OECD, 2010; Olsen, Lie, 2011).

The European Union is aware of the need to synchronize education with the social and cultural context of the reality we are living in. This is why it places considerable emphasis on technology education, as the social and cultural bases of education are strongly influenced by the rapid development of new technologies and the broad infiltration of information and communication technologies into each area of human life (EU, 2001; Králik, Tinley, 2017; Ambrozy, Valčo, Bhattarai, 2017). Reforms carried out by European countries in the context of the European Union recommendations and attempts to build a knowledge society should contribute to the reinforcement and improvement of the status of technology education in relation to the position of relevant school subjects within the curriculum as well as in relation to the young people's attitudes toward technology and science subjects. Unfortunately, it is not uncommon for changes introduced within the reforms to not function as intended; they have neither fulfilled expectations and nor have they brought about the intended improvement.

2. TECHNOLOGY EDUCATION AT BASIC SCHOOLS IN SLOVAKIA

In Slovakia, primary and lower secondary education (ISCED 1 and ISCED 2) is organized as a nine-year-long single-structure system, in which primary education lasts four years and lower secondary education lasts five years. Primary and lower secondary education takes place at so-called basic (elementary) schools, with nine grades, where children start to fulfil their compulsory school attendance at the age of six. A basic school consists of first and second stages. The first stage of a basic school is composed of grades 1 – 4 and the second is composed of grades 5 – 9.

Technology education has always been part of the general education provided at basic schools. Until 1948 it was carried out by means of training for manual work, which included work skills and mainly training in simple manual skills. In the form of the school subjects *work education* and *technical education,* taught in grades 1 – 4 (first stage of basic school) and 5 – 9 (second stage of basic school), it continued until 1997. After the year 1960 the freestanding school subject *work education* was taught with an allocation of one lesson per week in grades 1 – 3 and two lessons per week in grades 4 – 5. In grades 6 – 9 the lesson allocation was three lessons per week in each grade. But consequently (1960 – 1997) the lesson allocation was gradually decreased, finally to 60% (Lukáčová, Bánesz, 2007).

Under the influence of the former Soviet Union, which was a strong ideological role model for Central and East European countries in those times (the so-called Eastern or Communist Bloc as the Soviet Union and the aligned countries of the Warsaw Pact were named), high social status was prescribed to workers and a great emphasis was placed upon manual workers in particular. Consequently, great attention at basic schools was paid to preparation of students for manual trades.

After the political changes in 1989 (the so-called Velvet Revolution in Czechoslovakia in 1989; the dissolution of Czechoslovakia into two separate independent states, the Czech Republic and Slovakia, in 1993) humanization of education become a dominant priority of the national education system. Decentralization and humanization of the education system were accompanied by an emphasis on foreign-language teaching, while technology education became unattractive and surplus to requirements. An erosion in social awareness of the importance of the basic principles of technology for both society as well as human life resulted in an environment in which:

- subjects relevant to technology education (*work education* and *technical education*) at basic schools were taught increasingly by unqualified teachers (teachers specializing in other subjects);
- very often teaching subjects relevant to technology education did not follow their curricula;
- financial and material support of the subjects was reduced step by step;
- young people's interest in technical fields of study and employment and technical professions decreased significantly.

Due to the various problems in the system of education which had led to the aforementioned state of affairs, a changed approach in relation to technology education appeared in 1997. From this year, at least a formal declarations of the necessity to support technology education and to develop the technological literacy of children and youth have been formulated by relevant public bodies.

Paradoxically, just at the time when in Slovakia technology education was being neglected, in most European countries it was being significantly reinforced in the shape of different educational reforms. One of the most significant initiatives has been the *Recommendation of the European Parliament and the Council on Key Competences for Lifelong Learning* (EP, 2006). In this document basic competences in science and technology are included among eight so-called key competences, i.e., competences which all individuals need in order to succeed in a knowledge society, for their personal fulfilment and development, and for active citizenship, social inclusion and employment. Competence in technology is viewed as the application of knowledge and methodologies in response to perceived

Strategy Versus Reality in Technology Education ... 69

human wants or needs, including understanding changes caused by human activities and the related responsibility of each person (citizen) for these changes. Based on the fact that "competence" is understood as a construct consisting of relevant knowledge, skills and attitudes, competence in technology should comprise:

- knowledge of the basic principles of the natural world; fundamental scientific concepts, principles and methods; technology and technological products and processes;
- understanding of the impact of science and technology on the natural world; advances, limitations and risks of scientific theories; applications of technology in societies at large (in relation to decision-making, values, moral questions, culture, etc.);
- skills in using and handling technological tools and machines as well as scientific data to achieve a goal or to reach an evidence-based decision or conclusion; the ability to recognize the essential features of scientific inquiry and communicate the conclusions and reasoning that led to them;
- an attitude of critical appreciation and curiosity, an interest in ethical issues and respect for both safety and sustainability (in particular as regards scientific and technological progress in relation to oneself, family, community and global issues).

The incorporation of competences in science and technology among the key competences proclaimed by the European Parliament resulted from social needs and actual developments in science and technology. It might be assumed that these social needs and developments in science and technology would also have created a supportive environment for the social acceptance of the value of technology in Slovakia and that this would result in the reinforcement of technology education at schools, including basic schools (as a precondition for the creation of conditions for sustainable industrial and economical social development). But the Slovak reality was different (Hašková, 2015; Hašková, Dvorjaková, 2016; Hašková, Manduľáková, Van Merode, 2017).

Before 1996, the subject *work education* was taught with a lesson allocation of two lessons per week at each grade of the second stage of basic school (equivalent to lower secondary education – ISCED 2). The content of the subject consisted of three independent parts, which were technical education, agricultural work and family education. This state of affairs changed twice, first in 1996 and secondly in 2008. The first change consisted of renaming the subject *work education* to *technical education* and the number of lessons allocated to it was decreased from two lessons per week to one lesson per week, still in each grade of lower secondary education. The next change was performed within the curriculum reform that came into operation through enactment of the new Law on Education in 2008 (Law No. 245/2008).

The most significant feature of the curriculum reform in 2008 was the introduction of the so-called State Education Program and School Education Programs. Via the reform, the government guarantees basic education by means of the State Education Program which is compulsory for all basic (primary) and secondary schools. Based on the State Education Program, schools create their own School Education Programs. A School Education Program consists of the compulsory State Education Program plus optional school subjects which constitute approximately 30% of teaching time, according to the needs of the school or region, or requirements of the students and their parents. These lessons do not need to be devoted to new optional school subjects as they can also be used to enhance teaching of some of the compulsory subjects included in the State Education Program. Another change brought about by the reform, connected with the form and structure of the newly created education programs, was the definition of educational areas for each level of education. As regards technology education, the previously mentioned school subject *technical education* was renamed *technology* and was incorporated into the educational area *Man and the World of Work* consisting of three subjects: *manual training* (the first stage of basic school), *world of work* and *technology* (the second stage of a basic school):

- *manual training*   4th grade   –   1 lesson per week
- *world of work*   7th grade   –   0.5 lesson per week
     8th grade   –   0.5 lesson per week
- *technology*   7th grade   –   0.5 lesson per week
     8th grade   –   0.5 lesson per week

This means that the lesson allocation for technology education (subject *technology*) was cut from 1 lesson per week to only a half of a lesson per week taught only in the 7th and 8th grades, or the school could determine the grade in which the subject was taught (ŠVP ISCED 1, 2008; ŠVP ISCED 2, 2008; ŠPÚ, 2008).

Legislatively prescribed changes started to be introduced into practice at the beginning of the academic year 2008/2009 and were completed in 2012/2013, when the teaching process in all grades 5 – 9 was already being carried out in accordance with the new School Education Program.

In practice, implementation of the curriculum reform was accompanied by strong criticism (Hašková, Bánesz, 2015), and not only in relation to the reform of technical education but also in relation to other school subjects. Calls for a systematic solution to the reform's failings resulted in the introduction of a readjustment of the State Education Program. A new, innovated State Education Program entered into force in September 2015 (ŠPÚ, 2015). Positive aspects of the new innovated State Education Program have brought significant improvement to technology teaching and its position at schools. In accordance with the innovated State Education Program, technology is taught currently one lesson per week in all grades (5 – 9) at the second stage of basic school. Moreover, there was also elaborated a system of standards for the particular grades.

According to the new Innovated State Education Program (ŠPÚ, 2015) the purpose of the subject technology is to guide students toward acquisition of basic skills and competences in different labor-related activities, to contribute to students' deeper understanding of the various jobs and professions connected with the subject of technology, to lead to their familiarization with the labor market and ultimately to the development of students' life and professional orientation.

The content of the subject is based on specific life situations in which people come into direct contact with human activity and technology in its diverse forms and wider contexts and, through technical achievements, protect the world and their cultural heritage. The concept of the subject is based on the practical activities of students. The subject is focused on skills and habits useful for students' future lives in society, using creative thinking and co-operation among students.

The content of the subject matter is intended for all students regardless of gender. Students learn to work with different materials and devices, acquire basic working skills and habits, and develop creative technical thinking. When developing the designs and creation processes of products, they combine practical skills with creative thinking. The subject enriches the basic education of students with an important component laying the foundations of the field of technology that are indispensable for further study and the functioning of people in real life. Students learn to plan, organize and evaluate their work independently and also in a group. They are guided to adhere to the principles of safety and hygiene at work. Depending on the age of the students, a system is developed that provides students with important information from the world of work and helps them to make responsible decisions about their future professional orientation and decision-making in life.

The basic tasks of the subject technology (ŠPÚ, 2015) include:

- teach students to distinguish and safely use natural and technical materials, tools, and equipment;
- teach students to adhere to established rules and to adapt to altered or new tasks and working conditions;
- teach students to experiment with ideas, materials, technologies, and techniques;
- form suitable and appropriate habits of students for family life;
- develop students' sense of responsibility for their health, interpersonal relations and finances as well as for the convenience and security of their immediate surroundings and environment;

Strategy Versus Reality in Technology Education … 73

- develop students' sense of responsibility for the quality of their own and their joint work output;
- develop students' basic working skills and habits in different work-related areas;
- teach students how to plan and organize their work and use appropriate tools, instruments and aids at work, and in everyday life;
- lead students to perform their basic tasks persistently and consistently, apply creativity and their own ideas in their work and efforts to achieve quality results;
- form students' basic attitudes and values in relation to work and the environment;
- develop students' perception of work and work activities as opportunities for self-realization, self-actualization and the development of entrepreneurial thinking;
- teach students to orient themselves in different fields of human activity and forms of physical and mental work;
- develop students' knowledge and skills necessary for their employment, choice of professional career and further professional and life orientation.

The above-mentioned tasks clearly point to the fact that the subject of technology is characterized by significant specificities compared to other general subjects taught at basic school. The specifics of technology relate mainly to its focus on the practical activities of students and development of their manual skills. In order for the subject to fulfill its mission, it is necessary for schools to have specially equipped classrooms – school workrooms designed for the practical teaching of technology. The essence of the work in school workrooms is to teach students how to handle and work with different tools, devices and various types of materials, develop their skills in this direction, teach them to adhere to work habits and work safety and lead them to designing and making their own products, both on their own and in group work (Serafín et al., 2016; Valentová – Brečka, 2017).

3. ROLE OF TECHNOLOGY EDUCATION IN NATIONAL EDUCATION POLICY

Following a statutory order of the National Council of the Slovak Republic (parliament), the government of the Slovak Republic was obliged before the end of March 2013 to elaborate an *Activity Status Report on the Education System and Systematic Steps for its Development*. This document was commissioned to grant the Slovak education system a vision of its long-term development and a conception of the relevant systematic steps toward that development. Although then minister of education Dušan Čaplovič (4. 4. 2012 – 3. 7. 2014), an antecessor of ministers of education Peter Pellegrini (4. 6. 2014 – 25. 11. 2014), Juraj Draxler (26. 11. 2014 – 23. 3. 2016), Peter Plavčan (23. 3. 2016 – 31. 08. 2017), Gabriela Matečná (1. 9. 2017 – 12. 9. 2017) and the current incumbent Martina Lúbyová (13. 9. 2017), had prepared the first draft of this document and submitted it for consultation and in September 2013, after incorporation of recommendations resulting from the consultation, submitted a final draft to the government for interdepartmental consideration (MŠVVaŠ SR, 2013), the report has never been put into the schedule for government discussion.

The document has not been submitted to the government despite a request submitted by the signatories of the *Declaration of the Trade Union of Workers in Education and Science of Slovakia*, an independent, apolitical and non-profit organization established in accordance with Law No. 83/1990 on the Association of Citizens (OZ PŠaV, 2016) and Stakeholders in Education to Support the Quality of Education and Science in Slovakia (OZ PŠaV, 2016). The signatories of the declaration even before the parliamentary election held in March 2016 had asked all political parties standing as candidates for the National Council of the Slovak Republic (as Slovakia's parliament has been called since 1992; NR SR, 1996; NR SR, 2018) to promise that before the end of the year 2016, in co-operation with the stakeholder institutions, they would prepare and authorize a *National Strategy for the Development of Education and Training*, which would be based on the *Activity Status Report on the*

Education System and Systematic Steps for its Development (MŠVVaŠ SR, 2013).

As a fulfilment of this requirement one can cite a document called the *National Development Program of Education and Training "Learning Slovakia"* submitted for consultation by the previous minister of education Peter Plavčan in October 2016 (MŠVVaŠ SR, 2016). The document, elaborated by a group of experts nominated by the Ministry of Education, Science, Research and Sport of the Slovak Republic, described the framing of a program of changes planned by the ministry to be achieved within the scope of a long-term, 10-year timeframe. According to this document, the main goal of education and training was to be a balanced fulfilment of the needs and demands of individuals and society. Its authors mentioned that Slovakia had not yet responded adequately to the challenge of the transition from an industrial to information society as well as to the impact of new technologies on the need for new skills. In the manufacturing sphere, traditional skills, tools and machining techniques have retreated in the face of new requirements in terms of digitization, automation and the growing importance of additive manufacturing. However, this has not been reflected adequately in the vocational training offered by the regional education system. For this reason vocational education and training in Slovakia has become the subject of serious and increasing criticism for a prolonged period of time. Dissatisfaction has mainly been related to the insufficient level of practical technical training, which has resulted from the insufficient and out-of-date material and technical equipment of secondary vocational schools. Within this context the authors of the national program *Learning Slovakia* have emphasized the need to analyze the expected impact of the information society on the required knowledge, skills, abilities, attitudes and workforce habits relevant in the context of the Slovak Republic, and the need to recognize specific skills and competences which can be applicable more widely in different jobs and positions, with respect to changing conditions in the near future. The stated goal of increasing the proportion of training carried out in a manufacturing environment by means of dual education and forming agreements between schools and employers can be understood as a strategy for addressing the content of technology education in schools.

The conceptual framework of the national program addresses only the need for interconnection of vocational education and training provided by secondary vocational schools (ISCED 3) with the needs and requirements of employers and practice. The need to promote the interconnection of vocational technology education carried out at the lower level of secondary education (ISCED 2) with technology education carried out at elementary (basic) schools, and the need to analyze possible necessary changes in the content of technology education in basic school, is not mentioned. Partially this could be a result of the fact that in 2013 (only three years before the design of the national program *Learning Slovakia*) the curriculum reform of basic schools was completed and the authors of the national program had not dealt with the curriculum issue. This problem is pointed out also by Miron Zelina (2016), the co-author of previous school reforms. Evaluating the conception of the national program *Learning Slovakia* he draws attention to the fact that in the document no goals in terms of changing education content are mentioned, and this refers to changes in the content of education in general, not specifically the content of technology education. Furthermore, in his opinion the submitted document lacks any information on why similar intentions of previous reform proposals had not been implemented or why they had not had the expected positive impact on practice.

From our point of view a weakness in the presented conception is also the absence of any comprehensive description of the current state of the system of education and from it resulting identification of the most serious problems. In this regard the *Activity Status Report on the Education System and Systematic Steps for its Development* (MŠVVaŠ SR, 2013) had been considerably more specific. The Activity Status Report also drew attention to the deepening youth interest in vocational education and training, accompanied or even strengthened by the reduced number of lessons of practical education at lower secondary education (i.e., in the case of Slovakia at basic schools). In relation to the curriculum reform (2008 – 2013) it drew attention to the fact that the introduction of School Education

Strategy Versus Reality in Technology Education ... 77

Programs designed at the level of each school should contribute to increasing students' preparedness for real life, including enhancing their employability in the labor market (as the School Education Programs should take into consideration the specific needs of a particular school, derived from the parents' requirements and needs of local employers, as well as from the interests of the students and other stakeholders), but in practice their creation faced a lot of problems. Redistribution of curriculum design (specification of education content) from the national to the school level was not carried out consistently and schools only took partial advantage of their new autonomy and responsibility. To a great degree it was a consequence of the insufficient resources and technical equipment of schools, a lack of didactic teaching materials and finances, problems with assurance of teaching by qualified teachers as well as weak construction and clarification of the strategic intention and purposes of the curriculum reform and absence of teacher training targeted at the development of the skills necessary to design curricula and elaborate School Education Programs.

As a strategic aim for the development of regional education the *Activity Status Report on the Education System and Systematic Steps for its Development* announced a sufficiently funded and effectively functioning system of regional schools, available to all social classes and providing quality education and training responding to current and anticipated needs of practice. Quality education assurance was linked to several pillars, among which the two most important were quality of teachers and content of education.

In the context of the discussed issue, the most important strategic goals included in the systematic steps for the development of the education system were the intention to support further development of regional education and the intention to take measures to support the interest of basic school students in vocational training in accordance with labor market needs.

Analyzing both documents (the national program *Learning Slovakia*, MŠVVaŠ SR, 2016; Activity Status Report, MŠVVaŠ SR, 2013), we agree with Pupala's view (2016) which considers the methodology of the conception of the national program *Learning Slovakia* to be questionable because (unlike the Activity Status Report) the program presents goals stated for the education sphere but it does not mentioned neither indicate how these goals should be reached. Moreover there are specified no basic contexts following of which settings of the stated goals was done.

4. THE REALITY OF TECHNOLOGY EDUCATION IN PRACTICE

4.1. Purpose of Research

The education policy of the European Union calls for the support of school development, and the modernization and improvement in quality of education. In accordance with the policy of the EU, in its *Reports on the State of the Education System and Systematic Steps for its Development* each Slovak government has announced a national education policy and within it significant attention has been paid also to technology education at all levels of education. Despite some differences in the government announcements, each of them has declared support for further development of vocational education and increasing pupils and students' interest in it, in accordance with labor market needs.

To find out the reality, i.e., to find out how the education policy announcements related to technical education and relevant legislation have been reflected in practice, and in particular to find out their impact on teaching practice at basic schools (lower level of secondary education) field research was carried out. The research was based on semi-structured personal interviews with technology teachers working at basic schools in a research sample of which all regions of Slovakia were represented. As the research results show, despite the proclaimed good intentions of the different national strategies, programs and reforms, the reality is different.

4.2. Methodology

In education and sociological research, survey research is a frequently used method (Fraenkel, Wallen, 1993; Jaeger, 1988). In survey research information is gathered through asking questions. Answers to these questions given by a broader research sample of respondents constitute the research data of the consequent research study whose goal is to reveal certain attributes of a studied issue. This means that in survey research a broader group of people is asked about their opinions, attitudes, beliefs, knowledge and experiences regarding the issues under investigation. To allow respondents to express their opinions, attitudes, beliefs, knowledge and experiences freely, the questions should be formulated in a broader, more general way, not too specific or guiding respondents to some particular answers. An alternative strategy for defining survey questions is to use a hierarchical approach, i.e., to begin with the broadest, most general questions and to end with the most specific ones.

The main question of our research was which topics (thematic units) should be included in the curriculum of the school subject technology taught at basic schools in Slovakia (according to ISCED, this means the lower level of secondary education and in the Slovak context, the second stage of basic education) to ensure fulfilment of its mission and not to suppress in practice its meaningfulness and value in the formation of students' attitudes to work, i.e., formation of students' choice of their future professional career (Pavelka, 2016; Avsec, Jamsec, 2016; Fujikawa, Maesako, 2015). A subsequent research question asked how the curriculum reform came up with the fulfilment of the subject mission. To find answers to these questions meant:

1. identifying redundant topics (thematic units) taught within the technology subject curriculum;
2. identifying topics (thematic units) relevant to the subject technology, supporting its mission (i.e., to approve the curricular attributes of the subject);

3. assessing the impact of the curriculum reform on the subject's teaching, i.e., on its curriculum and forms of its realization.

Taking into consideration that the intention of the survey research was to focus on a deeper qualitative analysis of the issue under study (Bogdan, Biklen, 1992), questioning by means of personal interviews was used (Seidman, 1991).

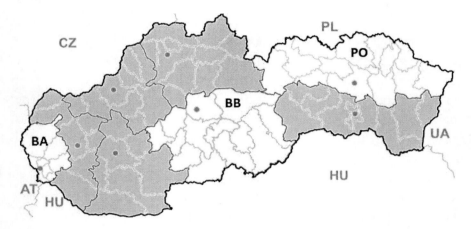

Figure 1. Regions where personal interviews were carried out (BA – Bratislava region, BB – Banská Bystrica region, PO – Prešov region, AT – Austria, CZ – Czech Republic, HU – Hungary, PL – Poland, UA – Ukraine).

The target group of the questioning comprised technology teachers. In order to obtain objective answers to questions aimed at curricular aspects and forms of teaching the subject technology before and after the curriculum reform (before the curriculum reform the school subject was named *technical education*; after the reform the school subject was *technology*), there was a requirement for the interviewees to have been in teaching practice for a longer period of time.

As the results of pilot research focused on schools' attitudes towards technology teaching and the prominence given to this subject at basic schools – carried out by Manduľáková (2016) – showed significant differences among particular regions of Slovakia, it was necessary to include in the research sample technology teachers from all regions of

Strategy Versus Reality in Technology Education ... 81

Slovakia. With respect to the difficulties of using personal interviews, it was problematic to bring together a research sample of teachers that would be representative of the whole of Slovakia and also difficult for the research group to travel around the whole country. The final solution was to carry out personal interviews with groups (representative research samples) of teachers from three regions of Slovakia, in particular these were regions of Bratislava (BA), Banská Bystrica (BB) and Prešov (PO), representing the west, center and east of the country (Figure 1). A description of the research sample is presented in Table 1.

Table 1. Numbers of teachers interviewed per region

	Region			Total
	Bratislava	Banská Bystrica	Prešov	
Number of teachers	26	20	24	70
- male	9	4	8	21
- female	17	16	16	49
Practice > 10 years	5	4	2	11
Practice > 20 years	21	16	22	59

As Table 1 shows, in total 70 semi-structured interviews were carried out. In these interviews teachers expressed their opinions and experiences related to:

- changes in realization of technical education at their schools caused by the curriculum reform (i.e., changes between teaching the school subject *technology education* before the reform and teaching the school subject *technology* after the reform);
- ideal state of technology teaching (what the teachers imagine under "an ideal state" as regards teaching; how and under what conditions would they like to teach it);
- further necessary changes (following the curriculum reform what the teachers consider to be necessary to do furthermore in relation to teaching technology; what changes should be made), or from

82   *Alena Hašková and Silvia Manduľáková*

their point of view which further changes would enhance the quality of technology teaching at their school;

- curricular aspects of the subject technology (what should and what should not be incorporated into the curriculum of the subject technology).

Data from the interviews consequently underwent a qualitative analysis, focusing on the frequency of content units and categories and their intensity.

4.3. Research Results and Discussion

The results of the qualitative analysis of the personal interviews were processed separately for each group of respondents, i.e., separately for groups of teachers in-service in the particular regions of Bratislava, Banská Bystrica and Prešov.

Survey Results – Bratislava Region

Teachers in the Bratislava region coincide in their opinion that the technology curriculum should be focused first and foremost on the thematic units of technical materials and machining. As a reason, they assert that this knowledge is as an integral part of general technical education. Most serious reservations related to a lack of respect for cross-curricular relationships, which occurs in both State Education Programs as well as in School Education Programs. A frequently cited example of this phenomenon was the incorporation of the thematic unit Electro-technology into the education programs (a difference of two grades: in the subject technology this thematic unit is taught in the 6th grade, while in physics it is taught in the 9th grade of basic school). But teachers in general hold the view that teaching and managing electro-technology is significantly difficult and demanding for an age group comprising basic school students. Further there is a consensus that thematic units dealing with financial literacy of students should move from technology to math, and thematic units dealing with computer literacy (how to use and work with ICT) should be moved to the subject information technology (informatics). To ensure the adequate quality of technical education for youths, the teachers called for the involvement of secondary school teachers (ISCED 3) in discussions on curricula for basic schools.

A general consensus among the interviewees was also recorded as regards the form of teaching technology. The teachers stated that subject matter content is very demanding to prepare both in terms of teaching activities, relevant materials and technical equipment. But at the same time the teachers declared their belief that each topic should be taught in a practical way, and more demanding thematic units should be accompanied by excursions.

An interesting result of the survey was a finding that arose in the discussion on what was the ideal way to teach technology; the teachers did not mention thematic units or topics which should be (or should not be) taught. What they mentioned was simply the provision of resources and technical conditions appropriate to practical activities which should be used in teaching technology. In our opinion this finding does not prove teachers' contentment with the curricula of the subject. Altogether, some measure of their discontent is proved by the above-mentioned comments and remarks as regards the education programs. What it is evidence of is the insufficient standard of school facilities to provide opportunities for teaching technology predominantly in a practical way, which means the idealized goals of teaching this subject become deformed in practice. A result of this state of affairs was that the interviewees, on being asked to present their visions of the ideal way of teaching technology, dealt at first with the issue of ideal conditions to ensure practical forms of teaching. They dealt with necessary premises for technology teaching (specialized classrooms, workrooms), required equipment (technical kits, tools and devices, technical apparatuses, materials necessary to make various products), an efficient funding model to ensure materials necessary for practical activities which should be carried out in teaching particular topics, and a need to improve in general the very low status of the subject (especially when regarding it in the context of other school subjects, and when regarding the unstable position of the subject in the State Education Program, and the underestimation of the importance of the subject by parents).

In assessing the curriculum reform, the interviewees very often expressed the opinion that the reform was not prepared sufficiently. From their point of view the reform should have started with the creation of the necessary conditions for its realization. To these conditions they include mainly the furnishing of specialized classrooms for technology teaching (workrooms) and ensuring of materials necessary for practical activities (this is in accordance with their vision of the ideal form of technology teaching). After this teacher in-service training was to be carried out, and only then were curricular changes to be implemented into practice. Within the context of teacher training for the implementation of new curricula, the respondents expressed very critical views also as to the familiarization of teachers with the intentions of curriculum reform. It was not an isolated opinion that many teachers had not yet grasped the main intention of the reform. Interesting opinions were stated also in the context of the assessment of the current state of technology teaching, such as statements in which the teachers characterized the technology teaching process as unstable (not in general, only particularly in relation to schools at which they taught). Although the teachers assessed the repeated increase of the compulsory number of technology lessons positively (Innovated State Education Program valid from September 1, 2015; ŠPÚ, 2015), they drew attention to the fact that until the spatial, material and technical conditions of teaching the subject improved at schools, no adequate quality of its teaching could be expected (regardless of the lessons allocated per week to this subject or particular topics included in its curriculum) and at the same time no adequate quality of students' technical skills could be expected, either. The teachers would have been pleased if the Ministry had realized the introduction of the changes on the basis of closer communication and co-operation with schools.

Survey Results – Banská Bystrica Region

Teachers in the Banská Bystrica region, similarly to the teachers in the Bratislava region, assessed the incorporation of thematic units focused on technical materials into the State Education Program in a positive way and had reservations about the thematic unit Electro-technology. Most serious reservations were about the incorporation of the theme of logical circuits into the curriculum. Teachers suggest that this be removed from the State Education Program. In regard to cross-curricular interaction of the subject technology with physics, the teachers drew attention to the incoherence and uselessness of some of the topics, and also in the case of electro-technology to its difficulty for students.

A paradoxical finding is that in the teachers' view no further major changes are necessary, despite the fact that the changes already performed are considered to be uncoordinated and ignoring of teachers' opinions. If some changes are to be made, the teachers consider it would be beneficial and efficient not to support changes in the curriculum but to support the content of the course together with the provision of proper resources and technical conditions (equipment) necessary for its teaching at schools.

In accordance with the results of the inquiry performed in the Bratislava region, at the question of the ideal form of technology teaching also the interviewees in the Banská Bystrica region in their responses to this question declared as a priority the need to ensure adequate conditions for technology teaching so that its focus would be on the practical activities of students and not on theoretical forms of teaching the subject.

Contrary to the Bratislava region, the teachers in the Banská Bystrica region:

- stressed very specifically the need to develop students' manual skills in the context of different practical activities;
- called more strongly for methodological support for teachers;
- linked their requirement to stabilize the subject with a particular requirement to assign technology as a compulsory subject in all grades 6 – 9 with the allocation of two lessons per week in each grade;

- in relation to the ideal form of teaching technology stated also the availability of textbooks of high quality written for particular grades (instead of the one elaborated for all grades, as has been done, whose quality is in their opinion unsatisfactory).

In their assessment of the impact of the curriculum reform on the realization of technical education at basic schools the teachers in the Banská Bystrica region also didn't focus on curricular aspects but in a very spontaneous way commented predominantly on the conditions of teaching the subject. They pointed to the fact that due to the reform conditions had become notably worse, as the reform and the State Education Program introduced in 2008 (ŠVP ISCED 1, 2008; ŠVP ISCED 2, 2008; ŠPÚ, 2008) prescribed cuts to the minimum compulsory lesson allocation of technology teaching, and together with financial reasons, led the school heads of many basic schools to make the decision to liquidate established equipped workrooms and to use these rooms for other purposes (mainly for teaching information technology and foreign languages).

Content analysis of the teachers' statements following the content category of space and material conditions for technology teaching detected two aspects related to teaching technology. Although insufficient (or even absent) ensuring of appropriate space, material and technical conditions for technology teaching obstructs the work of teachers and logically decreases the quality of the technical education provided by schools to students, this cannot be considered the cause of technology's low status. From the interviewees' point of view, the low status of technology results from the minute "juggling" of the subject within the system of general education subjects and from the many who question the need for this subject as a compulsory one at basic school, and the associated low social support given to this subject. In many cases the teachers drew attention to the fact that this perception of the subject's status is consequently reflected in attitudes and mainly decisions of the school leadership (or it significantly influences their attitudes and decisions). Half of the interviewed respondents in the Banská Bystrica region linked the subject's status directly to the school leadership.

From the point of view of subject status and its social perception, the teachers clearly considered the situation to have been more favorable before the curricular reform.

Survey Results – Prešov Region

Although the results of the interviews performed in the Banská Bystrica region led to some differences in comparison with the results obtained for the Bratislava region, in the Prešov region the differences with the other regions were even more marked.

Results of the interviews in the Prešov region, analogous to the results obtained in the Bratislava and Banská Bystrica regions, again point to the controversial insertion of the thematic unit Electro-technology into the technology curriculum. A particularity of this region was the very strong requirement of the respondents to focus the content of the technology curriculum on development of practical activities in the handicrafts area. The respondents evaluated the currently taught thematic units as irrationally sequenced and moreover very difficult for students of that age (mainly the above-mentioned Electro-technology mentioned by all three regions; besides the call to exclude this unit from the technology curriculum there were also calls to relocate it to the physics curriculum). With difficult topics students very often experience feelings of failure and frustration, and in the teachers' opinions technology should be mainly about experiences.

Technology teachers assess their workload in technology lessons as higher than the workload of other subject teachers (including their own workload when teaching a subject apart from technology). With regard to topics which require practical activities, to complete the course of a technology lesson is more difficult in terms of time, materials and methodologically. This is why they propose teaching technology in smaller groups of students.

A further particularity of the Prešov region was that at the same time as the call to divide classes into smaller groups of students for technology, there were also calls to separate boys and girls or to introduce into the technology curriculum topics that should be taught separately for girls and boys.

As in the case of the two other regions, respondents in the Prešov region connected the ideal form of technology teaching with creating and ensuring "ideal" conditions for its teaching – with modernization of school facilities, equipment of schools with appropriate materials, tools, devices and teaching aids, establishment of storage rooms besides workrooms, establishment of specialized classrooms equipped with computers (ICT), provision of proper teaching materials and in-service teacher training (continuing education opportunities), and an increase in the number of compulsory lessons of technology at particular grades of basic school (in many cases two lessons per week was stated as an ideal number).

It is disputable to which extent some of the respondents' remarks were objective (e.g., in descriptions of the ideal form of technology teaching). It might be that some subjective feelings of "discrimination" in comparison with the other regions (or in particular with the Bratislava region) could be felt (respondents had no cognizance of the selection of the regions in which the survey research was carried out, i.e., the comments were based on respondents' general feelings and were not influenced by disclosure of said information).

While the respondents in the Bratislava and Banská Bystrica regions evaluated the impact of the curriculum reform on technology education carried out at basic schools in general in a negative way, teachers from the Prešov region considered the situation as more or less unaffected. However at this point it is necessary to warn that "unaffected" means that from the teachers' point of view the reform did not bring any significant (either positive or negative) changes and "everything is carrying on as before". But "everything is carrying on as before" means a continuation of the negative development of the realization of technology education at schools, which the reform failed to stop and has not reversed yet (i.e., the reform did not stop a falling-off in technology teaching conditions and these are continually getting worse as they had been getting worse before the reform). In this context the respondents expressed their apprehension of the further development of the position of technology within the education programs as well as of the further development of technology education at basic schools. On the one hand the respondents consider the reality of technology teaching at schools to be out of step with the labor market, but on the other hand they appreciate at least the effort to improve something, e.g., the innovation of the State Education Program introduced from 1 September 2015 (ŠPÚ, 2015).

As the factor analysis shows the most marked recorded differences between the Bratislava and Prešov regions in relation to the subject of technology are as follows:

- higher criticism and almost rejection of the subject recorded in the Bratislava region; in the Prešov region significantly higher acceptance of the subject;
- although teachers in both regions approach the subject critically (with regard to insufficient resources for its teaching and a lack of material and technical equipment at schools), schools in the Bratislava region (basic schools in general, including their leaders, not only technology teachers) do not feel any greater need to change this situation, they would rather place emphasis on foreign language teaching – by contrast teachers in the Prešov region are characterized by a strong will to cope with the low status and poor conditions of technology teaching and, despite them, teach the subject in a way that might be as interesting, attractive and beneficial for students as possible, and which would offer the students as many opportunities for practical activities as possible;
- in the Bratislava region technology was primarily considered a supplementary subject which although in the past had a justification and was important (because of the manual and technical skills acquired), nowadays it has lost this justification (technology is understood as an additional subject offered to students simply to increase their morale in the context of other more theoretical subjects); in the Prešov region despite the unfavorable conditions the teachers exercise greater care and

diligence in teaching the subject to an adequate level, as they want to give their students a practical chance in the labor market;

- a tendency of parents to call into question the status of technology and its relevance was significantly the highest in the Bratislava region where the parents very often assumed a negative attitude towards the expectation of the school that their child will perform some manual activities, as they expect their child will be a lawyer, doctor or manager.

To illustrate the above-mentioned, we choose several examples from the responses of the respondents from the Bratislava region:

- *It is necessary to set the State Education Program in a different way. Technology does not fulfill the purpose (mission) of the subject.*
- *It is a question whether it is worth teaching this subject at all.*
- *I consider the subject overall as a negative.*
- *Technology should only be an optional subject.*
- *The subject should be restful, relaxing.*
- *Why should we produce something? We in Bratislava can buy everything at the Chinese supermarket for one euro. Let the others elsewhere learn technical skills and handicrafts; here in the capital it doesn't make sense. Technology should explicitly only be an optional subject.*

CONCLUSION OF SURVEY RESEARCH IN THE CONTEXT OF LABOR MARKET NEEDS AND REQUIREMENTS

The adaptation of educational institutions to the demands of their "customers" means adapting what they offer them not at the output stage but at the input stage. Adaptation of schools to the demands of their "customers" means that schools are logically amenable to their customers' demands for education services (or to the preferences their customers have

Strategy Versus Reality in Technology Education ... 91

– the notion "school customers" covers in general both students and their parents). Unfortunately, it does not mean that schools are amenable to the requirements of the potential employers of their graduates. Schools' strategies are largely determined by their system of funding, in the context of which the quality of school graduates is not critical to school budgets. What is critical for school budgets are the numbers of students enrolled in schools (i.e., not the quality of their graduates but quantity of enrolled applicants) and meeting the preferences of students and their parents for particular study programs but not the preferences of potential employers of graduates. Paradoxically, a school strategy of ensuring graduate quality could create an existential problem for a school. These facts were reflected to a great extent in the interviews carried out with technology teachers teaching at basic schools, regardless of the region they teach in. When considering the transition of basic school students to higher secondary schools, many interviewees mentioned the fact that students' parents have often framed their own vision of their child's future and do not want to be advised on the choice of the right secondary school or higher education institution for their child. More than a half of the respondents directly stated that the parent is the decision-maker and that parents' significantly prefer grammar schools. However very often this preference does not follow any logical or rational reason, but instead such reasons as "if s/he is accepted, let s/he has a better education" are given. And the practice is such that usually children are accepted independently of their knowledge, skills and previous school achievements.

- *Today's children have obscured moral and ethical values. They like and want to work manually, but only for some reward. I think this is the influence of their parents.*
- *The current trend is that students apply predominantly for grammar schools and business academies. But these are not decisions of students according to the school but according to their parents' wishes.*
- *Parents make decisions. I feel sorry for children who study something they do not like.*

- *Unfortunately, students graded 4* (sufficient, in a 5-grade scale with 5 meaning unsatisfactory) *are usually accepted to study at grammar school.*
- *Currently it is a trend: grade 4 students also attend grammar schools! Everybody wants to be very smart!*

Besides the aforementioned general decrease in the status of technology, parents significantly contribute to the degradation of the structure of the school system in Slovakia (Vantuch, 2015). The professional focus of higher secondary schools in all regions is unsystematically adapted to the preferences, interests, requirements and needs of parents. Due to this fact the network of secondary vocational schools does not correspond to the economic needs of the particular regions and to the requirements of the regional labor market and employers acting in it. In this context a surplus of students at non-technical (non-vocational) higher secondary schools is increased markedly by the growth of the capacities of art schools and private schools, which are predominantly focused on arts and non-technical study programs.

Ensuring a labor-force structure corresponding in each region to labor market needs is a very difficult task and is definitely not simply a problem of education (of the regional education system). Schools simply create their development strategies following the demands of their customers and the customers' preferred study programs. It is a question how, within the declared national education policies to adapt the regional structures of schools to the needs and requirements of the regional labor markets, to force citizens to respect the regional labor market's needs taking into consideration their further professional orientation (Tomková, 2010; Lukáčová, 2014).

REFERENCES

Ambrozy, M., Valčo, M., Bhattarai, S. (2017). The Ethical Aspect of Scientific Interest in Selected Physical Theories. *Communications - Scientific Letters of the University of Žilina*, 4(19), 2017, pp. 79-84.

Avsec, S., Jamsec, J. (2016). Technological Literacy for Students Aged 6 – 18: a New Method for Holistic Measuring of Knowledge, Capabilities, Critical Thinking and Decision-Making. *International Journal of Technology and Design Education*, 1(26), 2016, pp. 43 – 60.

Bogdan, R. G., Biklen, S. K. (1992). *Qualitative Research for Education*. Boston, Allyn & Bacon, 1992.

Dopita, M., Grecmanová, H. (2008). Secondary school students and interest in natural sciences. *e-Pedagogium*, 8(4), 2008, pp. 31–46.

EU (2001). *Report from the Commission of 31 January 2001: The concrete future objectives of education systems*. Available from: http://europa. eu/legislation_summaries/education_training_youth/general_framework /c11049_en.htm.

EP (2006). Recommendation of the European Parliament and of the Council of 18 December 2006 on Key Competences for Lifelong Learning. *Official Journal of the European Union*, 2006/962EC, L 394, pp. 10-19. Available from: http://eur-lex.europa.eu/legal-content/EN/TXT/PDF/?uri=CELEX:32006H0962&from=EN.

Fraenkel. J. R., Wallen, N. E. (1993). *How to Design and Evaluate Research in Education*. USA: McGraw-Hill, Inc., 1993.

Fujikawa, S., Maesako, T. (2015). Present Situation and Problems of Technology Education in Japan: With Focusing on Technology Education as General Education. *International Research in Education*, 2(3), 2015, pp. 173–182.

Hašková, A. (2015). Technical education – Cinderella in a technology-based society? *INTED 2015*, *9th international technology, education and development conference, Conference proceedings*, pp. 90-98. Madrid: IATED Academy, 2015.

Hašková, A., Bánesz, G. (2015). *Technology at Basic Schools – Yes or Not*. Praha: Verbum, 2015.

Hašková, A., Dvorjaková, S. (2016). Analysis of Technology Education Development at Schools in Slovakia. *The European Proceedings of Social and Behavioural Sciences EpSBS*, Vol. VIII – icCSBs 2016, pp. 236–245. Future Academy, 2016. DOI: http://dx.doi.org/10.

94 *Alena Hašková and Silvia Manduľáková*

15405/epsbs.2016.05.24, http://dx.doi.org/10.15405/epsbs(2357-1330). 2016.5.

Hašková, A., Manduľáková, S., Van Merode, D. (2017). Problematic Aspects of Technology Education in Slovakia. *Communications: scientific letters of the University of Žilina*, 1(19), 2017, pp. 75–80.

Hus V., Aberšek, B. (2007). Early science teaching in the new primary school in Slovenia. *Journal of Baltic Science Education*, 1(6), 2007, pp. 58-65.

Jaeger, R. M. (1988). *Survey Research Methods in Education. Complementary Methods for Research in Education.* Washington, DC: American Educational Research Association, 1988.

Králik, R., Tinley, S. J. (2017). Kierkegaard`s ethics as an answer to human alienation in technocratic society. *Communications - Scientific Letters of the University of Žilina*, 1(19), 2017, pp. 25-29.

Lamanauskas, V., Gedrovics, J., Raipulis, J. (2004). Senior Pupils' Views and Approach to Natural Science Education in Lithuania and Latvia. *Journal of Baltic Science Education*, 1(5), 2004, pp. 13-23.

Law No. 83/1990 on the Association of Citizens. Available from: http://amavet.sk/download/kluby/dokumentacia/2010/zakon_o_zdruzovani_o bcanov.pdf.

Law No 245/2008 on Education. Available from: https://www.minedu.sk/zakon-c-2452008-z-z-o-vychove-a-vzdelavani-skolsky-zakon-a-o-zmene-a-doplneni-niektorych-zakonov-v-zneni-neskorsich-predpisov/.

Lukáčová, D. (2014). Requirement of companies on school graduates. *Trends in education,* 1(7), 2014, pp. 345-348.

Lukáčová, D., Bánesz, G. (2007). *Technology Education Transformations.* Nitra: UKF, 2007.

Manduľáková, S. (2016). Regional differences in technology teaching. *Mutual informedness – a way to efficient development of research and pedagogical activities.* Nitra: UKF, 2016, pp. 32–39.

MŠVVaŠ SR (2013). *Activity Status Report on the Education System and Systematic Steps for its Development.* Available from: file:///G:/

Strategy Versus Reality in Technology Education ...   95

Subory%20od%2006-05-2015/Publ/JTIE/Podklady/Správa%20o%
20stave%20školstva%202013.pdf.

MŠVVaŠ SR (2016). *National Development Program of Education and Training "Learning Slovakia"*. Available from: http://www.minedu.sk/tezy-k-narodnemu-programu-rozvoja-vychovy-a-vzdelavania.

NR SR (1996). Act of the *National Council of the Slovak Republic* No 350/1996. Available from: https://www.nrsr.sk/web/Static/en-US/NRSR/Dokumenty/rules_of_procedure.pdf.

NR SR (2018). *National Council of the Slovak Republic.* Available from: https://www.nrsr.sk/web/.

OECD (2010). *PISA 2009 Results: Executive summary*. Paris: OECD, 2010.

Olsen, R. V., Lie, S. (2011). Profiles of Students' Interest in Science Issues around the World: Analysis of data from PISA 2006. *International Journal of Science Education*, 1(33), 2011, pp. 97-120. DOI: 10.1080/09500693.2010.518638.

OZ PŠaV (2016). *Declaration of the Trade Union of Workers in Education and Science of Slovakia.* Available from: http://www.ozpsav.sk/sk/Aktuality/udalosti-oznamy/deklaracia-odboroveho-zvazu-pracovnikov-skolstva-a-vedy-na-slovensku-a-partnerskych-reprezentac.alej.

Pavelka, J. (2016). Developing Students' Select Competences during Technology, Physics and Mathematics Lessons at Basic Schools. *Journal of Technology and Information Education*, 2(7), 2016, pp. 76–92.

Pupala, B. (2016). *Weak dream about "Learning Slovakia"*. Available from: https://www.postoj.sk/18134/riedky-sen-o-uciacom-sa-slovensku.

Seidman, I. E. (1991). *Interviewing in Qualitative Research*. New York: Teachers College Press, 1991.

96 *Alena Hašková and Silvia Manduľáková*

Serafín, Č., Bánesz, G., Havelka, M., Lukáčová, D., Kropáč, J. (2016). *Transformation of technology education curricula in the Czech and Slovak Republic after the year 1989.* Olomouc: UP, 2016.

ŠPÚ (2008). *State Education Program.* Available from: http://www. statpedu.sk/clanky/statny-vzdelavaci-program.

ŠPÚ (2015). *Innovated State Education Progra*m. Available from: http://www.statpedu.sk/clanky/inovovany-statny-vzdelavaci-program.

ŠVP ISCED 1 (2008). *State Education Program for the first stage of basic education. Educational Area: Man and the World of Wor*k. Available from: http://www.statpedu.sk/sk/Statny-vzdelavaci-program/Statny-vzdelavaci-program-pre-1-stupen-zakladnych-skol-ISCED-1.alej.

ŠVP ISCED 2 (2008). *State Education Program for the second stage of basic education - lower secondary education. Educational Area: Man and the World of the Work.* Available from: http://www.statpedu. sk/sk/Statny-vzdelavaci-program/Statny-vzdelavaci-program-pre-2-stupen-zakladnych-skol-ISCED-2/Clovek-a-svet-prace.alej.

UNESCO (1974). *Revised Recommendation concerning Technical and Vocational Education adopted by the General Conference of UNESCO at its eighteenth session, Paris, 19. November 1974.* Available from: http://www.google.sk/url?sa=t&rct=j&q=&esrc=s&source=web&cd=1 &ved=0CDQQFjAA&url=http%3A%2F%2Fwww.unesco.org%2Fedu cation%2Finformation%2Fnfsunesco%2Fpdf%2FTECHNICA.PDF&e i=3FObUs34Kcms4ASO1YDwCw&usg=AFQjCNE-ARvhHCg hxI9K8z d5MXYJVQUNcw&bvm=bv.57155469,d.bGE.

Valentová, M., Brečka, P. (2017). Analytical comparison of technology education content at basic schools in Slovakia and Czech Republic. *Trends in Education*, 1(10), 2017, pp. 7-14. DOI 10.5507/tvv.2017. 002.

Vantuch, J. (2015). *Is the system of education a support or a barrier to progressive structural changes in the economy of Slovakia*? Bratislava: Ekonomy institute of Slovak Academy of Science, 2015.

Tomková, V. (2010). Vocational education of secondary school students in the Slovak Republic. *Cywilizacyjne wyzwania edukacji zawodowej:*

wybrane problemy kształcenia zawodowego w Polsce i na Słowacji. Rzeszów: Max druk - Drukarna medyczna, 2010.

Zelina, M. (2016). *Strong critique of the prepared reform of the Slovak system of education. The experts discover the discovered!* Available from: http://www.pluska.sk/rady-tipy/10/dalsia-reforma-skolstva-vazeni-ste-si-isti-teraz-nase-deti-neprepadnu-sutazi-so-zahranicim.html.

In: Science and Technology Education
Editor: Steffen Pabst

ISBN: 978-1-53613-717-0
© 2018 Nova Science Publishers, Inc.

Chapter 3

MALE AND FEMALE TECHNOLOGICAL TALENTS AND THEIR MOTIVATED BEHAVIORAL CHOICES DURING THE LAST TWENTY YEARS

Ossi Autio, PhD

Department of Teacher Education,
University of Helsinki, Helsinki, Finland

ABSTRACT

Gender-based segregation and falling recruitment for scientific and technological studies are common phenomena in all Nordic countries. Furthermore, a great deal of research has been done and a wide variety of programs has been developed to increase female participation in careers such as engineering and physical science. This chapter is connected with an earlier research that assessed technological competence among adolescents (Autio & Hansen, 2002). Later on, this study traced and interviewed the students, who achieved the best results in the measurement of technological competence twenty years ago. The aim of this present study was to examine how these three best males and females have progressed in twenty years. Are they working in technology as well or did they end up in other professions? Although we must be cautious about the conclusions because of the limited number of research subjects, the study shows that it is possible to predict students' potential for ending in a technological career. However, the process in making motivated behavioral choices in the area of technology seems to be much more complicated for technologically talented females than for males.

Keywords: technology education, technological competence, technological talent, motivated behavioral choices

1. Introduction

Despite the progress that girls and women have made in education and the workforce during the past fifty years, there are still certain scientific disciplines in especially engineering that remain overwhelmingly male. The number of women in technologically related professions is growing. However, especially at the upper levels of these careers men outnumber women. In elementary, middle, and high school, girls and boys take technology related courses in roughly equal numbers, and about the same amount of girls and boys leave high school prepared to pursue science and engineering majors at college. Yet fewer women than men pursue these majors. Women are much less likely than men to continue in technologically related studies. Women's representation in technology studies declines further at the graduate level. By graduation, difference is dramatic and women earn only 20 percent of bachelor's degrees in some technological areas, such as physics, engineering, and computer science. What is more the difference increases yet again in the transition to the workplace. This gender-based segregation and falling recruitment for scientific and technological studies are common phenomena at least in all the Nordic countries (Sjøberg, 2002). However, it is a paradox that the inequity is noticeable in Finland where for decades gender equality has been a prime educational goal.

This chapter is build on an earlier research which defined and assessed technological competence among adolescents (Autio & Hansen, 2002). The aim of this present study was to find out if it is possible to find some new viewpoints for an emotionally charged issue of technological inequity by using the Expectancy-Value theory. In addition, this study examined how the three best male and female students have progressed. Are they working in technology as well or did they end up in other professions? Another point of view was to determine the elements accounting for the participants' motivated behavioral choices in the area of technology. Finally, the researcher tried to highlight some differences within these elements between males and females. The main research questions were as follows:

1. Did technologically talented males and females end up in technological careers?
2. What were the main elements in test participants' motivated behavioral choices in the area of technology?
3. What is the main difference between male and female technological talents in making motivated behavioral choice in the field of technology?

The results from each participant interview are shown in a figure based on Eccles (2009) Expectancy Value Model of Motivated Behavioral Choice. The model indicates each person's motivated behavioral choices in the area of technology during their life. These figures based on the expectancy value theory will be explained in more detail later.

2. MOTIVATED BEHAVIORAL CHOICES

During the interviews, typical elements affecting motivated behavioral choices in the area of technology were identified. These were classified according to the Eccles (2009) Expectancy Value Model of Motivated Behavioral Choice. This theory has been one of the most important theories on the nature of achievement motivation, beginning with Atkinson's (1957) seminal work. Theory can be used as a conceptual framework for understanding how youth come to choose and pursue a given career (Wigfield & Eccles, 1992; Eccles, 2008). According to Expectancy-Value Theory, students' achievement related choices are mostly determined by two factors, expectancies for success, and subjective task values. Expectancies refer to how confident an individual is in his or her ability to succeed in a task whereas task values refer to how important, useful, or enjoyable the individual perceives the task. Empirical work (Trautwein, Marsh, Nagengast, Lüdtke, Nagy & Jonkmann, 2012) suggests that expectancies and values interact to predict important outcomes such as engagement, continuing interest, and academic achievement. Other factors, including demographic characteristics, stereotypes, prior experiences, and perceptions of others' beliefs and behaviors affect achievement related outcomes indirectly through these expectancies and values (Eccles, 2009).

Furthermore, the model conceptualizes the value an individual associates with a given career choice as based on complex web of influences deriving from personal characteristics and various social contexts (e.g., peer group, gender roles, parental expectations). The most recent model consists of several factors or themes including: a distal cultural milieu with the cultural stereotypes and behaviors of key socializers. In addition, individual's perceptions of emerging self-knowledge is generating future goals and shaping self-confidence. Furthermore, individual characteristics and experiences are important while making the interpretations of previous experiences. These elements are later turned out to the expectation of success and into subjective task values. Finally based on the experiences in life and complicated decisions between all the elements in the model, the individuals are making motivated behavioral choices.

3. STUDY METHOD

Case study research excels at bringing us to an understanding about a complex issue or object and can extend experience or add strength to what is already known through previous research. Case studies emphasize detailed contextual analysis of a limited number of events or conditions

Male and Female Technological Talents ... 103

and their relationships (Stake, 1995). It is correct that the case study is a detailed examination of a single example, but it is not true that a case study cannot provide reliable information about the broader class (Flyvbjerg, 2006).

The research was carried out as a qualitative case study (Merriam, 1988) and the data was collected from individual theme interviews. The interviews were first tape-recorded and transcribed. Themes were identified and the portraits of each subject established (Lightfoot, 1983). Later the data was analyzed using the content analysis methodology. The analysis was carried out by assessing which of the essential elements in the Expectancy Value Model contributed motivated behavioral choices in the area of technology during test subjects' lives. These findings were later classified according to the themes and were reported in the conclusions. Prior to the interviews, the researcher had a short e-mail discussion with each test participant about the concept technological competence and about the Expectancy Value Model of Motivated Behavioral Choice. Each understood that technological competence was defined in the study as an aggregate of three areas: knowledge, skill, and emotional engagement. In addition, they understood that Expectancy Value Model was just a starting point and as the interview was based on self-reports, there were no right or wrong answers in the conclusions.

4. STUDY PARTICIPANTS

The study group consisted of three males and three females. Four of them were born in 1980 and two of them in 1982, whom when tested for technological competence twenty years ago as students achieved the best results in boys' and girls' test groups. Despite the fact that skilled behavior underlies nearly every human activity, our understanding about the factors that contribute to the attainment of expertise in technology education is far from complete. However, some attempts to define technological competence have been made. For example, based on Dyrenfurth's (1990) and Layton's (1994) work, Autio and Hansen (2002) defined technological competence as an interrelationship between technical abilities in psychomotor, cognitive, and affective areas. A simplified model of technological competence is described in Figure 1.

The test subjects were selected according to overall accomplishment in all three areas. In the original test group twenty years ago comprising 267 participants, a number of boys and girls performed better in certain areas (e.g., technological knowledge), but did not succeed as well in the others. More information about the research and test instruments, etc. in the original study is available in Autio (1997); Autio and Hansen (2002). According to the test results twenty years ago, it was easy to conclude that the selected test subjects were technologically talented and what is more they were definitely talented enough to pursue on a technological career.

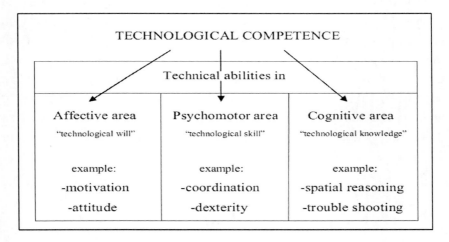

Figure 1. Technological competence.

The researcher had no previous knowledge of the test subjects' current employment status. Fortunately, the background of each test subject was somewhat different, but there were enough similarities in the elements behind their motivated behavioral choices in the area of technology to make some conclusions. The test participants were difficult to trace, but with the help of their old teachers, old school mates and the internet this was done after two months of investigation. The test participants were:

Male and Female Technological Talents ... 105

Subject 1 - academic technology researcher. He was born in 1980 and spent his school years in a rural village of about 4500 inhabitants in southern Finland approximately 150 kilometers north of Helsinki. He was exposed to technology education in primary and secondary school. In addition, he had an opportunity to take elective courses in technology education in upper secondary school, which was not typical in Finland 15 years ago. He lived with his parents, three brothers, and one sister. His father worked in forestry and mother was a homemaker.

Subject 2 - academic multi-talent. He was born 1980 in Helsinki which is the capital of Finland. His first school years were spent in a normal primary school, but at secondary and upper secondary level he studied at one of the highest ranked upper secondary schools in Finland. He lived with his parents and one younger brother. Both parents had earned Masters of Science in technology and both worked at the State Technical Research Centre. Many of his older relatives had also studied at the University of Technology.

Subject 3 - non-academic technology talent. He was born in 1980 and spent his school years in the same village as Subject 1. Both were exposed to technology education in the same primary and secondary schools. Following secondary school, he moved to a larger city with approximately 100000 inhabitants to study in vocational school. He lived with his parents and had two elder brothers and two sisters. His father worked as a taxi driver but was a main owner of a local bus company. His mother worked in a bank.

Subject 4 - from machine technology to an architect. She was born in 1982 and spent her school years in Helsinki area. She lived with her parents and a little sister. Her father had earned Master of Science in Technology (machine technology) and her mother was Master of Science in Economics and Business Administration. Her little sister was currently studying in Italy (bio information technology).

Subject 5 – academic single mother. She was born in 1982 and she spent all her school years in University training school in Helsinki area. She lived with her parents and sister. The family was just an ordinary

106   *Ossi Autio*

Finnish family with no academic degrees. Her father was a janitor and her mother was a homemaker, whom occasionally worked in a food store.

Subject 6 – technological talent with lower self-confidence. She was born in 1980 and spent her school years in Helsinki area. She had her primary education in a smaller school, but at the secondary level she moved to University training school. In the upper secondary school, she studied in a school which was concentrated in natural sciences. Her father was working in Helsinki city social department and her mother was a sole trader whom worked as an art director. In addition, her family consisted of an elder sister and a younger brother who was a talented electrician.

Two out of three male study participants had finished their studies at the University of Technology. The first was quite sure of his decision to choose a technology career already after secondary school, but the second was interested in several other areas as well. He could have chosen a number of other careers. The third test subject was equally talented in technical matters. Unfortunately, he was not particularly interested in other school subjects while being in comprehensive school; so he began to study computers and automation technology in vocational school instead of continuing in a more academic direction. Two out of three female study participants had also studied at the University of Technology. The first was quite sure of her decision of choosing a technology career already after secondary school, but the second had a lower self-concept related to technology and started her studies in the University of Technology a couple of years later. The third test subject was equally or even more talented in technical matters but mainly due to lack of self-confidence and encouragement of the main socializers she began to study economics in vocational high school instead of continuing in a more technological direction.

5. RESULTS

Each test participant's educational path related to technology is presented in the next section. The descriptions of the educational paths were based on the Expectancy Value Model of Motivated Behavioral Choice. The model was first introduced to the test subjects by e-mail and then discussed within the theme interviews in more detail. The elements of the motivated behavioral choices of each test subject are described more precisely in Figures 2-7. As the results were based on self-reports no absolute value was given to the strength of the particular elements.

Subject 1 – Academic Technology Researcher

Subject 1 finished school in 2000 with good grades (average of all school subjects 9.2/10.00). After finishing upper secondary school, he started computer science studies at the University of Technology. In 2005, he graduated with a Master of Science in technology and continued to doctoral studies in computer science and engineering. He finished his doctoral thesis in January 2010. He is willing to continue his research career and he will apply for a scholarship from the Finnish Academy. He assumes that his technological competence develops further in the projects he undertakes in the future.

Subject 1 became familiar with technology in early childhood, using Lego and constructing huts in the forest with his younger brothers. His father had worked with various tools fixing cars and machines at home. Subject 1 responded positively to technology education: already early in comprehensive school, craft and technology had become his favorite subject. He was also good in other subjects, e.g., mathematics and physics, but technology was of special interest. Particularly electronics and computers provided him with an increasing intellectual challenge.

Subject 1 was also gifted with his hands and so could concretely witness his own development in terms of things he produced, for example a metal detector and twilight switch. Yet he received the best encouragement from being able to understand how things work and being able to develop his own ideas. Although his internal feedback was usually enough, he still appreciated the positive and encouraging feedback from his technology teacher, because teachers in other subjects did not do the same.

Once the technology education courses were over, computers became Subject 1's main interest in upper secondary school. This provided him a new kind of challenge after working with wood, metal, and electronics. His competence in technology was further developed by these studies in computer science. Later, in his academic career, he concentrated on carrying out research in a supportive and challenging working environment, and despite relatively low salaries, after finishing his doctoral thesis he remains willing to continue his research career. The elements behind Subject 1's motivated behavioral choices are presented in Figure 2.

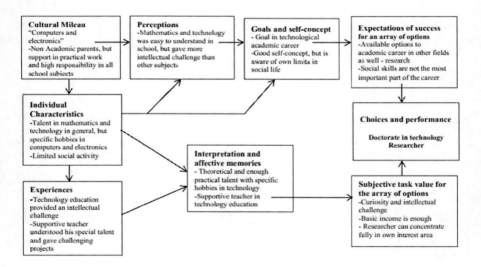

Figure 2. Elements behind Subject 1's motivated behavioral choices.

Subject 2 – Academic Multi-Talent

Subject 2 finished upper secondary school in 1999 with good grades (overall 9.4/10.00). As most of his school mates had very ambitious career plans, he was planning studies in medicine as well. However, after compulsory military service he decided to study automation technology at the University of Technology. In 2007, he completed Master of Science in technology and began working for an international company which manufactures hospital automation devices. He feels comfortable in his job, enjoys the innovative working atmosphere, and thinks that his technological competence will still improve in the future.

Subject 2 had become acquainted with technology in early childhood through familiarity with Lego and radio-controlled (RC) cars. His family was competent in technology and his mother in particular was very supportive, often fixing toys with the children. Subject 2's motivation was based on a child's curiosity and he wanted to know how toys worked. The teacher was also very competent and could create an open and atmosphere, while maintaining rational planning, investigation, implementation, and evaluation processes. It was easy to talk with the teacher, whose feedback was rewarding, and developed skills and technical thinking further.

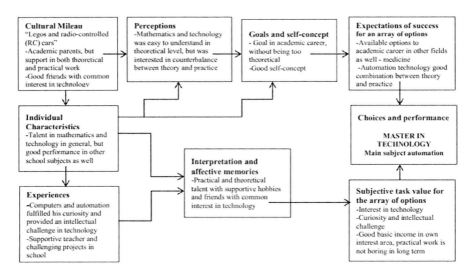

Figure 3. Elements behind Subject 2's motivated behavioral choices.

In upper secondary school Subject 2 had to concentrate more on academic subjects and was not at all sure that he would choose a technology-related profession in the future. He was interested in physics, chemistry, and mathematics, but still wanted to find a balance between theory and practice. Computers gave him a new chance to develop his technological competence without being too theoretical. This was one of the main reasons why he chose automation technology as his major subject at the University of Technology. Today he sees the inspiring and technically open environment of his work as the main factor in his development. As well, his good friends with a common interest in technology provide him with support and new ideas to develop his competence further. The elements behind Subject 2's motivated behavioral choices are presented in Figure 3.

Subject 3 – Non-Academic Technology Talent

Subject 3 finished secondary school in 1997. His grades were not particularly good (overall 7.3/10.00) and instead of choosing an academic career and upper secondary school, he began to study computers and automation technology in vocational school. After finishing in 2000, he did his compulsory military service where he had an opportunity to work with optical cables and computers. He also became interested in the mechanics of tanks and other vehicles. He began his studies in automation technology in polytechnics and in 2005 he graduated as an engineer and started working in an engineering office as an electrical wiring designer. In his current post in an international mining and construction company – he feels comfortable and enjoys the innovative working atmosphere.

Subject 3 had become familiar with technology in early childhood, using Lego and emulating his elder brothers. There was plenty of stimulation at home. His father had good facilities for working on cars, tools of all kinds, and available machines. At least he thinks, there was no significant increase in his competence during primary school as he had seen his elder brothers working with real cars, there was nothing interesting in making wooden toys. In secondary school, however, electronics in particular provided him a challenge and he generally felt much better as he had more freedom and his choices were respected by the teacher; this was not the case with several other school subjects.

Male and Female Technological Talents ... 111

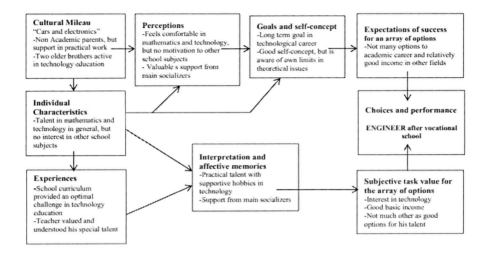

Figure 4. Elements behind Subject 3's motivated behavioral choices.

Subject 3 was gifted with his hands so he could concretely witness his own development in the products he produced (e.g., an infrared light gate and metal detector). He felt comfortable in technology education classes, but his technological competence developed even more through his hobbies than through school. When he was older and more skillful his two elder brothers allowed him to repair cars with them as a respected co-worker and not just a pain in the neck.

After finishing secondary school Subject 3 went on to study in vocational school. This presented him with a new kind of challenge as he could concentrate on areas of special interest and develop his technological talent. Later his competence in technology was developed by his studies in automation technology. Although he was not especially good in several school subjects during his earlier school years he graduated from polytechnic school near the top. In his current post in an international company, he feels he could have learned more languages at school, but his choice of moving straight into vocational school was the best decision in terms of his talent and interests. According to him, how his technological competence develops in the future will depend on interesting and challenging future projects. The elements behind Subject 3's motivated behavioral choices are presented in Figure 4.

Subject 4 – From Machine Technology to an Architect

Subject 4 finished school in 2001 with good grades (average of all school subjects over 9.0/10.00). After finishing upper secondary school, she started to study machine technology at the University of Technology. However, after five years she changed her major to Architect. Currently, she is working in an architect office and having a couple of years to finish her degree.

Subject 4 had become familiar with technology in early childhood, using Lego but she played with Barbie as well. Subject 4 responded positively to technology education: already early in comprehensive school and she was interested in how things work in general, but any products were not especially interesting. The teacher was capable although the test subject thought that he was a little bit frightening for a small girl. Furthermore, she had no friends with the same interest area to join her in technology education lessons. His father was a good role model, but she did not get much support for her technological talent as father was not at home too often because of his work. In any case, the support from her main socializers was limited and in upper secondary school she noticed her technological talent mainly because he was good in mathematics, not because of her accomplishment in technology.

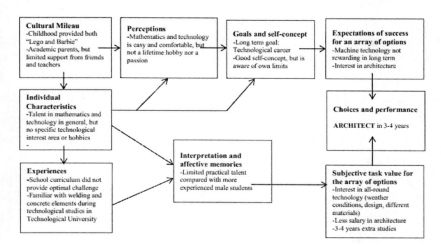

Figure 5. Elements behind Subject 4's motivated behavioral choices.

Yet she received the best encouragement from being able to understand how things work in everyday life. Her self-confidence in technology was high and actually she did not need much support as she felt comfortable in the technological world. While her later studies in machine technology she got more experiences in real life technological environment. She became acquainted with welding and making concrete elements. She felt comfortable but noticed that her skills were limited at least when compared with other students who had much more experience from the technological world during their hobbies. Anyway, she thought that her competence in technology developed but she had no passion for any special phenomena in technology. Furthermore, she had no technologically related hobbies to develop her competence further. In the long term, to study machine technology seemed to be meaningless to her future. Because of this, she decided to change her major and started studying to be an architect. As she was a woman of diverse talent, she felt this area much more rewarding to herself. She could fulfill her technological interest with different points of view: design, different materials, weather conditions and sociological elements. As she had finally found a technological area that suits her talent, she is willing to accept 3-4 years of more studies and even lower salary. Her choice corroborates with the idea that women seem more likely than men to be involved in, and to value, competence in several activities simultaneously (Baruch, Barnett & Rivers, 1983). The elements accounting for Subject 4's motivated behavioral choices are described in Figure 5.

Subject 5 – Academic Single Mother

Subject 5 finished school in University training school 2001. The school was one of the highest ranked upper secondary schools in Finland. She was good in several school subjects and graduated with good grades (average of all school subjects about 9.3/10.00). After finishing upper secondary school, she started to study computer science 2002 in vocational high school. However, as the studies were not as practical as she expected, she found out quite soon that this was not what she wanted to do for the rest of her working life. In the year 2003 she changed to study environmental technology in a smaller town close to Helsinki area in vocational high school. She felt comfortable in her studies and noticed her technological talent and finally she had enough self-confidence to take part in the qualification exam of technological University in Helsinki. In the year 2004 she started to study material technology in the technological University. Currently as single mother she has had some breaks in her studies, but she thinks she could graduate as a Master of Science in Technology in 1-2 years. However, she still wonders that her life as a single mother would be much easier if working as a veterinarian, which was her childhood dream.

Since her early childhood Subject 5 has been involved in technological area as her father always made renovations or was working with cars. Fortunately, she was the favorite girl of her father and she could join him in all the work he was doing as a janitor. Subject 5 also had an opportunity to take some extra technology education lessons while studying in upper secondary school; especially she enjoyed the internal combustion engine course. The teacher was encouraging and like-minded and she thought that her self-confidence grew up when she could show the boys that her skills and knowledge in technological area were remarkable. In addition, she has always felt comfortable in analytical thinking required in technological area. However, she has never had any specific aims or specific hobbies regarding to technology. To develop her technological competence further she thinks that she still needs continuous encouragement as her self-confidence in real life is still limited.

Currently, she is in the middle of hard decisions. As a single mother her life could be much simpler while working as a veterinarian. She thinks that she could organize her daily routines much easier by having a private practice. On the other hand, she could finish her studies in material technology and graduate as a Master of Science in Technology in 1-2 years. Although she thinks that her ability suits well in her current study area, she knows that in technological area a diploma is not enough – updated knowledge is required all the time. While working as a veterinarian as much updating training is not needed. Her choice is consistent with the statement that mathematically talented woman go into the biological and medical sciences instead of physical sciences and engineering (Vida & Eccles, 2003). The elements accounting for Subject 5's motivated behavioral choices are described in Figure 6.

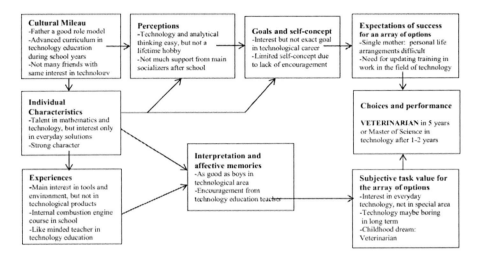

Figure 6. Elements behind Subject 5's motivated behavioral choices.

Subject 6 – Technological Talent with Lower Self Confidence

Subject 6 finished school in 1999 with good grades. From her opinion, she was good in all subjects but felt especially comfortable in mathematics. After finishing upper secondary school, she started to study business economy in vocational high school, but she thought that personnel management was not what she was waiting for her working life. Soon she changed her plans and in the year 2004 she graduated Bachelor of Business Administration. Since that, she has worked in several posts as an office assistant and as a contract coordinator. She feels there is enough challenge in her working life.

Subject 6 had an opportunity to join technology education classes in secondary school and she thinks she could have been successful in that area. However, there were no friends with the same interest, no encouragement from the teachers, parents and other main socializers. The main problem for her was that her self-confidence and social skills were limited and she could not consider technology education studies further as boys were too domineering in that area. Anyway, she finished a couple of good projects for example a flower watering device, but she felt she wanted more discussion from technological phenomena, not just the product. Sometimes the lessons were chaotic with loud voices from the machines and the restlessness of the whole working group. She thinks that special technology education lessons just for girls would not have been so troubled.

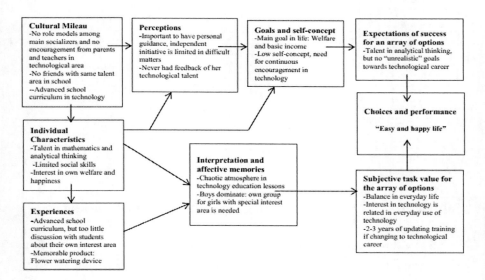

Figure 7. Elements behind Subject 6's motivated behavioral choices.

Although she had opportunities and enough talent to develop her technological competence further, without any support and with limited self-confidence considering a technological career was never an option. In mathematics, for example the feedback was much more positive and she knew her position from several exams. Anyway, her mathematical talent is valuable in her current duties and she feels comfortable everywhere analytical thinking is required. However, growing in her work on her

Male and Female Technological Talents ... 117

current post is the most important thing for her right now and she has any specific goals in her life. Although, she has always thought that her analytical skills would have been valuable in technological area as well, easy life with basic income and welfare is enough for her. Being unaware of her technological talent she did not even consider a technological career as she thought that these options were not realistically available to her. The same phenomenon is quite common as reported by Eccles (2008). The elements accounting for Subject 6's motivated behavioral choices are described in Figure 7.

CONCLUSION

This study tried to find out: *Did technologically talented males and females end up in technological careers?* The research showed that four out of six test participants were currently studying or had finished their studies in Technological University. In addition, one test subject has graduated as an engineer. One test participant was equally or even more talented in technical matters but mainly due to lack of self-confidence and encouragement of the main socializers she did not end up in a technological career. Based on these findings, we can assume that it is possible to predict student potential for a career in technologically related professions. However, the process in making motivated behavioral choices in the area of technology seems to be much more complicated for technologically talented females than for males and we can just imagine – how difficult the decisions would be without the talent.

The next study question was: *What were the main elements in test participants' motivated behavioral choices in the area of technology?* According to Eccles (2007) the kinds of educational and vocational decisions that might underlie gender differences in participation in physical science and engineering would be most directly influenced by individuals' expectations for success and the importance or value individuals attach to the various options they see as available. In this study, it was seen that many elements have an influence on the motivated behavioral choices in the area of technology already long before the test participants consider expectations for success or give value to the options they see as available. Consistent with the most recent simplified version of the Expectancy value model of motivated behavioral choices (Eccles, 2009); cultural milieu, individual characteristics and previous experiences seemed to be the main elements in the beginning of the process in motivated behavioral choices. If these elements are not in balance, the individuals' do not actively, or consciously, consider the full range of objectively available options in making their selections. What is more, many options are never considered because the individual is unaware of their existence or the individuals think these options are not realistically available to them (Eccles, 2008).

In the measurement of technological competence twenty years ago the test participants were found to have technological talent and it was easy to conclude that the selected test subjects' individual characteristics were suitable for a technological career. According to Byman (2002), students usually prefer and choose subjects and tasks, in which they are proficient and can show their competence. In addition, Eccles (2009) predicts that people select those activities for which they feel most efficacious or for which they have the highest expectations for success. Furthermore, Betz and Hackett (1986) demonstrated a link between the ratings of personal efficacy in various academic subjects and career choice. In addition, all six test participants had an opportunity to join technology education lessons in a school with advanced technology education curriculum. Although, the curriculum was not always optimal when providing technology for young girls, all test participants had experiences in the field of technology and were at least aware of the existence to consider this option as available. What is more, the schools were clearly aware of the gender role and cultural stereotypes. During the interviews, none of the test participants mentioned these elements as negative features. Vice versa all of them mentioned that they had positive feedback about their mathematical talent and they were not stereotyped as nerds or as a people with little direct human relevance.

The third study question was: *What is the main difference between male and female technological talents in making motivated behavioural*

Male and Female Technological Talents ... 119

choice in the field of technology? The issue of cognitive sex differences in technological competence remains hotly contested. The difference in technological knowledge, especially in spatial reasoning is consistent with some other researches (Linn & Petersen, 1985; Voyer, Voyer & Bryden, 1995; Autio, 1997; Autio & Hansen, 2002). It is stated that spatial skills are considered important for success in engineering and other scientific fields. However, we must take into account that spatial skills consistently improve with a simple training course and they are mostly due to previous experience in design-related courses such as technical drawing, as well as play with construction toys such as Legos (Sorby & Baartmans, 2000). In addition, according to Hyde, Lindberg, Linn, Ellis and Williams (2008) difference in average math performance between girls and boys no longer exists in the general school population.

What is more, women who enter technological university tend to be well qualified. Female and male first year students are equally likely to have taken and earned high grades in the prerequisite math and science classes in high school and to have confidence in their math and science abilities (Brainard & Carlin, 1998; Vogt, Hocevar & Hagedorn, 2007). Hence, in this study the main difference seemed to be that technologically talented females assessed their technological competence lower than males with the same achievements and held themselves higher standard believing that they had to be exceptionally successful in a technological field. This seems to be common phenomena in other technological subjects as well as can be conducted from Hill, Corbett and St. Rose (2010).

Another distinguishing element was the support from the main socializers in the field of technology as all female test participants reported limited support from parents, teachers or friends. Adolescents are especially concerned with a peer relationship and may be in special need of a close adult relationship outside of the home (Eccles, 2008). Reeve, Bolt, and Cai (1999) have shown that teachers who support students' autonomy in decision-making create more intrinsic motivation than those who intend to control their students. Support of autonomy is evident when an authority figure respects and takes the subordinate's perspective, promotes choices, and encourages decision-making (Ratelle, Larose, Guay, & Senecal, 2005).

Furthermore, parents, teachers and peers tell people what they are good at or not good at with very little information on which to base such conclusions (Eccles, 2009). Closely related to the effect of the main socializers seems to be social networking. With fewer friends in the same interest area, technologically talented females had limited supportive relationships. Prior research states that increase in social networking is predictive of increased job search intensity and many of the contacts assist career-directed behavior (Mortimer, Zimmer-Gembeck, Holmes & Shanahan, 2002). Furthermore, supportive relationships have been shown to facilitate adolescents' career exploration (Kracke, 2002). Thus, social connections can either directly support career entry, or play an important role by pointing out a feasible path toward career attainment that makes an individual better prepared to choose their career and establish an effective plan toward establishing that career (Shane & Heckenhausen, 2012).

Furthermore, emotionally supportive and an encouraging teacher-student relationship was mentioned with all male students as one of the main elements in developing their technological competence. This is consistent with Eccles (2007) who states that males will receive more support for developing a strong interest in physical science and engineering from their parents, teachers and peers than females. In addition, it is absolutely the case that all young people will see more examples of males engaged in these occupations than females. In a long term, this has a strong impact on self-confidence which is essential element when the individuals consider expectations for success or give value to the options they see as available in the field of technology and finally making motivated behavioral choices.

DISCUSSION

In this study, the three male and female students who had the best overall results in the measurement of technological competence twenty years ago were followed. Due to the long timeline, the study had obvious limitations: the research group was small and we can't be sure how well the participants remembered their pasts or did the researcher misunderstand some of the details during the interviews and in any case the self-reports are always quite subjective. In addition, the real action in making motivated behavioral choices is a much more complicated process than we can describe with a single figure.

It is easy to conclude that most of the differences between male and female can be explained by the support from the main socializers. Unfortunately, this seems not to be the whole picture. Most important elements that affected male participants' career decisions were technological talent, curiosity, interest and intellectual challenge. Other than talent, were not mentioned during the interviews with three best females and it was clearly seen that their interest was restricted in everyday technology not in special areas. Technology-related hobbies (e.g., Lego, computers, cars, and electronics) were definitely another very important element between males and females. It is quite obvious that technology related hobbies which were started early in the childhood had a positive effect on technological talent which for its part generated more interest and curiosity on technology related activities. After a while, these adolescents had much better self-confidence in technological matters. Obviously, this helped them to stay committed to a goal despite distractions and unexpected difficulties. In the end it was much easier to make motivated behavioral choices. In other words, as stated in Shane and Heckenhausen (2012) career-related personal control beliefs in primary control-contingent casual factors will lead an individual to extend a motivational engagement to pursue career-related goals.

Another fact seems to be that females are more likely than men to be involved in, and to value, competence in several activities simultaneously (Baruch, Barnett & Rivers, 1983) and that mathematically talented woman go into the biological and medical sciences instead of physical sciences and engineering (Vida & Eccles, 2003). Scientists are working to solve some of the most vexing challenges of our times: trying to find cures for several, tackling global warming, providing clean drinking water, developing renewable energy sources. In architecture, there are different views of design, different materials, weather conditions and sociological

Ossi Autio

elements. Engineers design many things for everyday use: mobile phones, computers, cars, wheelchairs, and X-ray machines. There are plenty of interesting areas in technology related studies and professional careers available for females. Attracting and retaining more women in these fields will generate more innovation, creativity, and competitiveness. However, females still make up a smaller number of students with technological interest from the start. A special concern is if we lose some of these technological talents later. The problem of the inequality in the field of technology seems to be far more complicated than we are used to think.

REFERENCES

Atkinson, J. (1957). Motivational determinants of risk taking behavior. *Psychol. Rew. 64,* 359-372.

Autio, O. (1997). *Oppilaiden teknisten valmiuksien kehittyminen peruskoulussa [Student's development in technical abilities in Finnish comprehensive school].* Research Reports No. 117. Helsinki: The University of Helsinki, Department of Teacher Education.

Autio, O., & Hansen, R. (2002). Defining and Measuring Technical Thinking: Students Technical Abilities in Finnish Comprehensive Schools. *Journal of Technology Education 14 (1)*, 5-19.

Baruch, G., Barnett, R. & Rivers, C. (1983). *Life prints.* New York: McGraw-Hill.

Betz, N. & Hackett, G. (1986). Application of self-efficacy theory to understanding career choice behavior. *Journal of Social and Clinical Psychology 4*, 279-289.

Brainard, S. G. & Carlin, L. (1998). A six-year longitudinal study of undergraduate women in engineering and science. *Journal of Engineering Education, 87*(4), 369–375.

Byman, R. (2002). Voiko motivaatiota opettaa? [Can we teach motivation?]. In Kansanen, P. & Uusikylä, K. (Eds.) *Luovuutta, motivaatiota, tunteita (25-41).* Jyväskylä: Gummerus.

Dyrenfruth, M. J. (1990). Technological literacy: Characteristics and competencies, revealed and detailed. In H. Szydlowski, & R. Stryjski (Eds.) *Technology and school: Report of the PATT conference (pp. 26-50)*. Zielona Gora, Poland: Pedagogical University Press.

Eccles, J. (2007). Where are all the women? Gender differences in participation in physical science and engineering. In Ceci, S. & Williams, W. (Eds.) *Why Aren't more Women in Science.* American Psychological Association: Washington, DC.

Eccles, J. (2008). Agency and Structure in Human Development. *Research in Human Development 5 (4)*, 231-243.

Eccles, J. (2009). Who Am I and What Am I Going to Do With My Life? Personal and Collective Identities as Motivators of Action. *Educational Psychologist 44(2)*, 78-89.

Flyvbjerg, B. (2006). Five Misunderstandings about Case-Study. *Research Qualitative Inquiry* 2006 (12), 219-245.

Hill, A., Corbett, C. & St. Rose, A. (2010). *Why So Few? Women in Science, Technology, Engineering and Mathematics.* AAUW: Washington.

Hyde, J., Lindberg, S., Linn, M., Ellis, A. & Williams, C. (2008). Gender similarities characterize math performance. *Science, 321*, 494–495.

Kracke, B. (2002). The role of personality, parents and peers in adolescents' career exploration. *Journal of Adolescence, 25,* 19-30.

Layton, D. (1994). A school subject in the making? The search for fundamentals. In D. Layton (Ed.) *Innovations in science and technology education* (Vol. 5). Paris: Unesco.

Lightfoot, S. (1983). *The good high school.* New York: Basic Books.

Linn, M. & Petersen, A. (1985). Emergence and characterization of sex differences in spatial ability: A meta-analysis. *Child Development, 56*(6), 1479–1498.

Merriam, S. B. (1988). *Case Study Research in Education: A Qualitative Approach.* San Francisco: Jossey-Bass.

Mortimer. J., Zimmer-Gembeck. M., Holmes, M. & Shanahan, M. (2002). The process of occupational decision making: Patterns during the transition to adulthood. *Journal of Vocational Behavior, 61(3),* 439-465.

Ratelle, C. F., Larose, S., Guay, F. & Senecal, C. (2005). Perceptions of parental involvement and support predictors of college students' persistence in a science curriculum. *Journal of Family Psychology 19,* 286-293.

Reeve, J., Bolt, E., & Cai, Y. (1999). Autonomy-supportive teachers: How they teach and motivate students. *Journal of Educational Psychology 91,* 537-548.

Shane, J. & Heckenhausen, J. (2012). Career-related goal pursuit among post high school youth. *Motivation and Emotion, 36(2),* 159-169.

Sorby, S. & Baartmans, B. (2000). The development and assessment of a course for enhancing the 3-D spatial visualization skills of first year engineering students. *Journal of Engineering Education, 89*(3), 301–07.

Sjøberg, S. (2002). Science and Technology Education: Current Challenges and Possible Solutions. In Jenkins, E. (ed.) *Innovations in Science and Technology Education Vol VIII*, Paris: UNESCO.

Stake, R. (1995). *The Art of Case Study Research.* California: Sage Publications.

Vida, M. & Eccles, J. (2003). Gender differences in college major and occupational choices. In Eccles, J. (2008) Agency and Structure in Human Development. *Research in Human Development 5 (4)*, 231-243.

Vogt, C. M., Hocevar, D., & Hagedorn, L. S. (2007). A social cognitive construct validation: Determining women's and men's success in engineering programs. *The Journal of Higher Education, 78*(3), 337–64.

Voyer, D., Voyer, S., & Bryden, M. (1995). Magnitude of sex differences in spatial abilities: A meta-analysis and consideration of critical variables. *Psychological Bulletin, 117*(2), 250-270.

Wigfield, A. & Eccles, J. (1992). The development of achievement task values: A theoretical analysis. *Devel. Rew. 12,* 265-31.

In: Science and Technology Education ISBN: 978-1-53613-717-0
Editor: Steffen Pabst © 2018 Nova Science Publishers, Inc.

Chapter 4

LEARNING SCIENCE IN THE SDGS ERA: OPPORTUNITIES FOR BUILDING YOUTH COMPETENCY

Seyoung Hwang[*]
National Youth Policy Institute, Sejong, South Korea

ABSTRACT

In this study, we propose a new vision for science education in the era of sustainable development goals. In the first section of the chapter, we discuss how the sustainable development goals (SDGs) identify new roles for science and technology to address global and local challenges such as climate change, energy innovation, and biodiversity. These areas of sustainability reveal new visions for science education by enabling us to approach science learning as a more community-based practice and collaborative way of thinking, beyond classroom-based learning. Based on this idea, the chapter presents 'youth sustainability competency' as an educational concept for identifying and discussing methods of promoting young people's engagement with SDGs issues. We also illustrate an example of such learning by focusing on a youth internship program in a community garden in New York City and a national youth center in South Korea. The focus of the analysis was to identify the elements of

---

[*] Corresponding Author Email: syh@nypi.re.kr.

youth sustainable competency and to discuss how youth engagement can be facilitated in ways which build youth competency through science and technology education while also addressing SDGs.

Keywords: sustainable development goals (SDGs), youth sustainability competency, youth, case study

1. A NEW ROLE FOR SCIENCE AND TECHNOLOGY IN THE SDGS ERA

In 2016, the international community took a significant step towards common prosperity and development of humankind for the next 15 years, according to the sustainable development goals (SDGs) proposed by the United Nations. The SDGs consist of 17 goals and 169 sub-goals that should be achieved for sustainable development. The content of the SDGs is the result of various efforts, including the debate on policies relevant to sustainable development over the past 40 years. The term "sustainable development" was first proposed in the 1987 United Nations Environment Programme Report, "Our Common Future" and is defined as "meeting the needs of the present generation without disturbing the ability of future generations to meet their needs (WCED, 1987: 1)." Since its inception, this concept has provided an important framework for the direction of social development in many countries. However, the debate over the meaning of sustainable development is still ongoing, and the ways in which sustainable development is implemented in the form of national policies, for example, have also diversified. The SDGs are meaningful because they present sustainable development as a developmental direction that the world should pursue. In other words, the SDGs provide a framework for the developmental direction of each country, taking into consideration each country's economic and social reality to achieve sustainability for that society. The SDGs also present the principles of inclusiveness and diversity and include consideration for cooperation between developed and developing countries and interrelationships among relevant sectors.

Learning Science in the SDGS Era: Opportunities for Building ... 127

In this era of SDGs, the role of science in addressing global challenges such as climate change, energy, health, and poverty, cannot be overemphasized, as summarized below:

> "Science is being challenged as never before as the world contends with the profoundly complex problems of living sustainably and equitably. That battle now has a common, global ambition – the 2030 Agenda – and if science is to support its achievement, it is vital that we share a common vision of the kind of science we need. It is science that is open and inclusive, that shares its benefits universally, and that makes a difference to real world problems not only by advancing our understanding, but also by contributing transformative societal responses. (Hackmann, Editorial, Environmental Scientist, September 2017)."

Accordingly, the science and technological innovations are especially expected to contribute to six themes, that are i) dignity relating to global poverty and inequality, ii) people specifically concerning health, education and gender equality, iii) prosperity in terms of sustainable economy, cities and resources, iv) planet including environmental issues such as ecosystem and global warming, v) justice for safe and peaceful societies, and vi) partnership to approach complex issues (Elsevier, 2015, pp. 16-21).

In the current discourse on sustainable development, today's youth have been identified as the responsible entities who will bear the future of the global community. As decisions made based on the interests of the present generations (such as environmental issues caused by economic growth) greatly influences the quality of life for future generations, the younger generations have the right and the duty to participate in the present social decision-making process. For example, this view is strongly reflected in the "UDNP Youth Strategy 2014-2017" set forth by the United Nations Development Programme (UNDP). The UNDP strategy positions youth as a sustainable future subject and aims for their empowerment. In particular, it emphasized that youth should be regarded not only as beneficiaries of the issue or policy but also as partners with equal rights, and they should be given opportunities to demonstrate their leadership. Therefore, the purpose of this chapter is to identify ways to promote youth competency by addressing SDGs-related issues through science education in the context of the lives of youth and the society in which they live.

2. LEARNING SCIENCE AS A WAY OF BUILDING YOUTH SUSTAINABILITY COMPETENCY

2.1. UNESCO Learning Objectives for SDGs

In 2017, UNESCO proposed learning objectives for each of the 17 goals. For example, with regard to SDGs 13 related to climate action, the learning objectives encompass knowledge on climate change and the social and ethical implications for climate change (see Table 1). For science education, this suggests a much wider learning scope than the traditional subject discipline, as it addresses not only the scientific knowledge on climate change but also ways of addressing climate change through science and various technologies. In more critical terms, incorporating SDGs into science education suggests going beyond technocentrism (Feinstein & Kirchgasler, 2014) and taking an interdisciplinary or transdisciplinary approach to learning about SDGs issues.

2.2. The Idea of 'Youth Sustainability Competency'

There have been various discussions in the field of environmental education and sustainable development education related to youth competency. One of the most widely-cited concepts is sustainability competence, which was used in Germany's sustainable development education project. Sustainability competence is defined as the "future-oriented ability to change and create future society by active participation based on sustainable development." Sub-factors include future-oriented thinking, an interdisciplinary approach, international society, understanding and cooperation regarding cultural diversity, participation,

Table 1. Learning objectives for SDGs 13 "Climate Action" (UNESCO, 2017, p. 36)

Cognitive learning objectives	The learner: • understands the greenhouse effect as a natural phenomenon caused by an insulating layer of greenhouse gases. • understands the current climate change as an anthropogenic phenomenon resulting from the increased greenhouse gas emissions. • knows which human activities – on a global, national, local and individual level – contribute the most to climate change. • knows about the main ecological, social, cultural, and economic consequences of climate change locally, nationally and globally and understands how these can become catalyzing and reinforcing factors for climate change on their own. • knows about prevention, mitigation and adaptation strategies at different levels (from global to individual levels) and in different contexts, and their connections to disaster response and disaster risk reduction.
Socio-emotional learning objectives	The learner is able to: • explain ecosystem dynamics and the environmental, social, economic, and ethical impact of climate change. • encourage others to protect the climate. • collaborate with others and develop commonly agreed-upon strategies to deal with climate change. • understand their personal impact on the world's climate, from both local and global perspectives. • recognize that the protection of the global climate is an essential task for everyone and that we need to completely re-evaluate our worldview and everyday behaviors.
Behavioral learning objectives	The learner is able to: • evaluate whether their private and job activities are climate-friendly and where to revise them if they are not. • act in favor of people threatened by climate change. • anticipate, estimate, and assess the impact of personal, local, and national decisions or activities of other people and world regions. • promote climate-protective public policies. • support climate-friendly economic activities.

future planning and execution, empathy and solidarity, motivation, and reflection (de Hann, 2006). Such sustainability competence is related to the capacity required to create a sustainable future and has recently been used in the development of several programs to support sustainable development education in universities.

The concept of action competence was developed from the Danish health and environmental education tradition, in which the term behavior does not refer to one specific behavior and instead refers to a variety of behaviors which all contribute to the pursuit of democratic values. Thus, action competence is related to democratic education. In addition, in terms of sustainability, this concept emphasizes the critical thinking processes of reflection and inquiry and pursues an optimistic vision of the future for the resolution of problems (Mogensen & Schnack, 2010). Next, reflective competency pursues "social change" more explicitly compared to action competence, and is discussed in the tradition of critical environmental education in South Africa. Reflectivity is a core concept that simultaneously leads to individual agency and social change and refers to a core competence necessary for understanding the assumptions behind behavior and decision-making. It supports the development of the ability to adapt to future changes, that is, the power to pursue sustainability (Lotz-Sisitka & Raven, 2009).

In recent years, UNESCO has highlighted the importance of understanding complex situations, creative and autonomous behaviors, and cooperation to achieve the SDGs. It has defined people with these competencies as "sustainability citizens" and presented core competencies they should embody. These eight core competencies focus on understanding the complexities and interrelationships of SDGs, communication, and creative resolution of issues through reflection and cooperation, based on environmental education and the discussion of ESD competency mentioned above and thereby addressing a higher level of goals. The core competencies of UNESCO's SDGs suggest the ultimate competency goals that citizens living in the SDGs era should embody in their communities instead of focusing on the development and characteristics of adolescence.

In this study, "youth sustainability competency" was defined from the viewpoints of the youths' competencies cultivated in the process of developmental tasks and the competencies necessary to achieve a sustainable society. It was broadly conceptualized into three categories: self-awareness competency, inquiry competency, and integrated problem-solving competency (see details in Hwang et al. 2017). This framework was basically developed to approach UNESCO's SDGs competencies and allow the extraction of concepts suitable for youth, as follows.

Table 2. UNESCO SDGs competencies (UNESCO, 2017: 10)

Components	Definition
Systems thinking competency:	the abilities to recognize and understand relationships; to analyze complex systems; to consider how systems are embedded within different domains and different scales; and to deal with uncertainty.
Anticipatory competency:	the abilities to understand and evaluate multiple futures – possible, probable, and desirable, to create one's own visions for the future, to apply the precautionary principle, to assess the consequences of actions, and to deal with risks and changes.
Normative competency:	the abilities to understand and reflect on the norms and values that underlie one's actions and to negotiate sustainability values, principles, goals, and targets, in the context of conflicts of interests, trade-offs, uncertain knowledge, and contradictions.
Strategic competency:	the abilities to collectively develop and implement innovative actions that further sustainability at the local level and further afield.
Collaboration competency:	the abilities to learn from others, to understand and respect the needs, perspectives and actions of others (empathy). to understand, relate to and be sensitive to others (empathic leadership). to deal with conflicts in a group, and to facilitate collaborative and participatory problem solving.
Critical thinking competency:	the ability to question norms, practices and opinions, to reflect on one's own values, perceptions, and actions, and to take a position in the discourse on sustainability.
Self-awareness competency:	the ability to reflect on one's own role in the local community and (global) society, to continually evaluate and further motivate one's actions, and to deal with one's feelings and desires.
Integrated problem-solving competency:	the overarching ability to apply different problem-solving frameworks to complex sustainability problems and develop viable, inclusive, and equitable solution options that promote sustainable development while integrating the abovementioned competences.

First, the self-awareness competency is related to the development of youth identity in a broader context. Existing youth activities focused on establishing and managing the goals of their activities, developing their self-identity and self-efficacy in the process, and seeking future careers; they were therefore limited to the personal context of youths' development process. In contrast, in the context of SDGs it is necessary to emphasize the viewpoints of the interaction by highlighting the various contexts in which the development of youth identity affects the sustainability of life, and affects areas such as education, health, environment, and safety. In this regard, the existing youth competencies include the concept of ecological resilience. For this study, we use the broader concept of resilience. The concept of resilience, which is often discussed in recent studies on youth well-being, can be defined as the "dynamic adjustment ability to positively cope with various environmental changes and stressful situations (Sewon Kwon et al., 2012: 40) (Hyein Jung, 2010; Sewon Kwon et al., 2012; Haase, 2004)." Sewon Kwon et al. (2012) empirically demonstrated that resilience was a major factor influencing the happiness of youth in Korea.

Table 3. Youth sustainability competency (Hwang et al. 2017: 40)

Components and Definitions	Sub-components
1. Self-awareness competency: the ability to reflect on one's personal identity on both community and global levels, and plan for the future	Self-identity
	Future-planning
	Resilience
2. Inquiry competency: the ability to actively investigate sustainability-related issues and alternatives	Critical thinking
	Reflective thinking
	System thinking
3. Integrated problem-solving competency: the ability to develop alternatives and take action on problem-solving with a culturally sensitive and collaborative mindset	Sympathy, sensitivity, respect for diversity
	Communication, leadership and fellowship, collaboration
	Creative problem-solving

Learning Science in the SDGS Era: Opportunities for Building ... 133

Second, the competency of inquiry was conceptualized based on the ability to understand and explore the complex and multi-faceted characteristics of SDGs in terms of basic life skills. The sub-components of this competency include critical thinking, reflective thinking, and systems thinking. Lastly, the integrated problem-solving competency emphasized the act of contributing to community problem-solving with regard to sustainability based on mutual understanding and cooperative values between different interest and sociocultural groups.

3. CASE STUDY 1: EAST NEW YORK FARMS YOUTH INTERNSHIP PROGRAM AND ITS SIGNIFICANCE TO SUSTAINABLE AGRICULTURE

3.1. Youth Engagement in Urban Farming

Urban farming contributes to the sustainability of a city through improvement of its environment and expansion of the production and consumption of local food. This is directly related to Goals 11 and 12 in the SDGs which call for the creation of sustainable cities and sustainable production and consumption. The East New York Farms Youth Internship program provides an opportunity for youth to contemplate how they will design their own futures by helping them recognize urban farming as a positive resource for their communities and teaching them about food justice. Located in one of New York's most decayed areas, Brookline, East New York Farms (ENYF) is a project that supports community gardens and uses local food as a means to contribute to increased sustainability in the community. ENYF operates an internship program for youth in their teens. The nine-month internship is comprised of new experiences including learning the fundamental knowledge required to grow a garden, cultivating real produce, helping with farm work in other gardens located in the area, and selling the harvested produce at the market. Through these experiences, interns cultivate a sensibility towards nature, recognize the significance of local food production and consumption, and gain the opportunity to observe community issues in a new light. The internship is not merely an opportunity to learn and experience work; it is also an opportunity for youth to communicate with their peers, initiate decision-making, gain a sense of emotional stability and achievement, and engage in self-reflection. Although the ENYF internship lasts nine months, youth continue their participation for two to three years. This can be viewed as a crucial element that contributes to the formation of a positive sense of self-identity in youth interns.

The ENYF internship program contributes to youth awareness of food justice issues in the local community. ENYF not only manages the internship program but also actively participates in local community food campaigns. ENYF is committed to positioning today's youth to be a driving force for leading strong change in the local community and increasing the influence of youth on the local community by organizing food justice campaigns. ENYF also participated in the organization of the Youth Food Justice Network. This network convened partner agencies throughout the Northeast areas for a learning, support, and information exchange. Furthermore, ENYF is actively involved in the nationwide "Rooted In Community National Network," which is a nationwide network that empowers youth to play a leadership role in their communities. At ENYF, youth and adults work together to create healthy communities and participate in various campaigns devoted to food justice through urban and rural farming, community gardening, food safety, and other relevant environmental justice topics. Local youth gain the knowledge and skills needed to support themselves and their communities at the annual national RIC Conference.

3.2. Promoting Youth Sustainability Competency through Urban Farming

In this portion, interview materials were utilized to explore the learning experience at the ENYF in terms of the idea of youth sustainability competency.

Learning Science in the SDGS Era: Opportunities for Building ... 135

[self-awareness competency: self-identity]

The youth internship is meaningful in that its youth gain an opportunity to develop self-identity through proactive exploration and relationships in a variety of contexts such as family, community, culture, and even the global environment. Through communication with their peers and area residents, youth are able to reflect on laziness, tardiness, interpersonal problems, passiveness, and other issues they may be facing. The youth mature as they learn to adapt to new situations.

I felt like this job really make me mature. I felt like when I got violations because violations, If I came in late or if did the wrong thing I feel like that actually built me because I knew my flaws and I knew those are areas that I could build in. (A)

I can use my street smart. So like you know help me get by. Because like that's what I've been using. I feel like this job built that too because me having to communicate with so much people someone different areas it helps me built up my street smart. So I know how to advocate for myself, I know how to speak to different people like all my teachers they're all different. I know how to go about them. When I'm not at school I just get a whole different vibe. I feel so different. When I come here since I build like a relationship for everyone here. (A)

For the youth, the internship experience provided a significant foundation for developing self-identity. Importantly, the internship has been an experience that supported youths' self-inquiry and the process of understanding and performing their role to make their local community sustainable.

Also, when returning to school I naturally talk with classmates about the meaning of gardening and importance of local food at the level I understand it. There might be some differences with other teens who pursue something 'cool', but I don't hesitate to show the 'farmer' side of me. (B, participant interview)

For me, I came out of my shell for the first three months when I first working here I didn't speak to anybody at all. I guess you could say social anxiety. I was afraid to speak to people. Because of this job it was like puts you out there and it makes you go and speak to people. It helped me a lot. Now I can talk to people (C, participant interview)

The small problems all teenagers have gradually improve, and my family was proud as they observed my transformation into someone with a positive self-image. Communication between the generations in my immigrant family also naturally occurred as we talked about produce. My mom like she really loves this and I think she loves me doing this for her benefit. She's like you come back with all the knowledge on how to of gardening it you know and you could teach me. She feels like it keeps me occupied like it keeps my mind on something positive. So she really likes this job. (A, participant interview)

[Self-awareness competency: future planning]

Thus, the youth were able to identify their strengths and weaknesses by steadily participating in internship activities for more than nine months, spending quality time with various people, and performing their assigned tasks. This experience with different communication styles provided an opportunity for them to reflect on their qualities as professionals.

It's for 9 months so it kind of gives you a little experience like say if you had a real job. Well this is a real job but like you know of future job as an adult you know it kind a because its lumpy. It is like an actual internship that goes on for 9 months so it gives us like you know of responsibility and you know for that specific in while in the time. (A, participant interview)

Being patient definitely because I want to be a psychiatrist. I got to be patient with people that seems differently from everybody around me. You don't think that average person. And I have to respect, listen and any like be patient. But here when I listen to people's problems and whatever I learn to not to judge. (B, participant interview)

I think its help. Like say after a surgery telling someone how to take care of themselves like especially with bathing like depending on. And it can also, I also considered like being a nutritionist because of this job. (C, participant interview)

[Self-awareness competency: resilience]

Learning Science in the SDGS Era: Opportunities for Building ... 137

The Brooklyn area was traditionally a slum in which crime and unemployment issues were chronic. Youth feel that living in this area is dangerous and not safe. However, the internship program helped youth identify the 60-plus community gardens that exist in the area. It also helped youth to develop an awareness of the positive resources in their community through opportunities to participate in a variety of health exchanges and activities during the program. Furthermore, gardening does not stop with the cultivation of fresh produce, and allows youth to become aware of the work they can do in their community for food justice. Through this exposure, youth in this area gain a more composed and positive mental state despite the bleak conditions of their communities and begin to proactively explore their own futures.

I learned that there's over sixty gardens in Eastern York. And this is my community. Like there is over sixty gardens in Eastern York itself. And I was just like wow that's so cool. Because like area that has violence apparently that has a lot of violence and all these things going on and a lot of crimes. And it's also positive things going on here. (A, participant interview)

I try to keep on positive mind. Unless someone just got shot on the news around the corner from my house then that's going to be on my mind. But if I'm just walking I just try to get positive mind and I always afraid in as God to keep me safe when I walk. But thinking about like what's the government and what's going on that's when I start to scare and fearful. What's going to happen in future or what's happening now. (A, participant interview)

I remember that I was struggling with my health because like before I came to this job I was borderline diabetic. So like after learning about how to take care about myself and I'm fine now. (C, participant interview)

[Inquiry competency: critical thinking, reflective thinking, system thinking]

The youth often return to school and naturally convey the meaning of gardening and the importance of local food to their peers at their own knowledge levels. The youth overcame their initial negative perspective on farming and proudly claimed this aspect of their identity by recognizing that they were different from their peers. In this process, they experienced reflective and systems thinking by revealing a critical awareness of peer culture, its pursuit of material values and fast food, and contemplating the relationship between health and food issues.

Environment. I definitely got interested in with the environment. About the whole food justice aspect of them like so I don't know. Ever since then I couldn't. If someone asks me about it I don't shut up I just keep talking about how it's like food justices is a form we've got to like we make together. (B, participant interview)

Easy living. Basically just material thing. I like video games and stuff like that. About here it's cool because you actually get to build like the bonds with people. (B, participant interview)

Teenagers like 13 and up to 17 they don't really come to the market to too much because like Queen said they used to process foods that you know of like fast foods. This is what they are used to of go grab a dollar beef patty. And that's not the best thing to eat to put in your body but they don't look at fresh as good. They just look at it as oh that's healthy I don't want to eat healthy food. (C, participant interview)

There's a lot of fruits and vegetables that I learn about. There's one Kohlrabi. I've never heard of it until I started working here and then my family always had to buy it every week. (C, participant interview)

[Integrative problem solving competency: communication, collaboration]

The internship program covers the development of social aspects such as getting along with peers and participating in decision-making in the community, in addition to the acquisition of knowledge and skills related to farming. During the internship program, youth participants may encounter struggles, conflicts, and difficulties in their peer relationships. However, the experience eventually helps them recognize their role in the community and learn how to act as a member of the community.

I became more open and more acceptable to people that cause a lot of people have a lot of different personalities. Everyone in the world has different personality so I had to you know cope with, dealing with different personalities in different people because at the market there's like a whole bunch of different customers and I have to hold my composure and stay professional and positive. So I felt like that actually changed my behavior outside of this job. (A, participant interview)

[At the conference,] I got to meet a lot of people there and you know when I was over there a new side of me came out that I never knew I had. Like the supervisor that went with me said that too she was telling me that I was like friendly I was outgoing. (B, participant interview)

4. CASE STUDY 2: NATIONAL YOUTH AGRICULTURE AND LIFE CENTER PROGRAM IN GIMJE

4.1. Integrating SDGs into Youth Programs Focused on Sustainable Agriculture

The National Youth Agriculture and Life Center in Gimje (hereafter referred to as the Gimje Center) is the only youth facility specialized in agricultural life in South Korea. Since its inception four years ago, its primary focus has been the promotion of youths' well-rounded development and awareness of sustainable agriculture through diverse experiential experiences of agricultural life science. It is expected to play a central role in promoting youth activity in these specialized areas. The youth activities are spread widely across sustainable agriculture (SDG2), sustainable development education (SDG 4.7), sustainable production and consumption (SDG 12), and climate change (SDG 13). The Gimje Center has been making efforts to develop specialized programs through the creation of agricultural, ecological, and experiential activities as a core theme of youth activities. The center considers agriculture to be the foundation of life and seeks to spread the value of sustainable agriculture as a countermeasure against changes in agriculture's ecological environment due to future food problems and climate change. While conventional agriculture has focused on the abundance of the harvest, the paradigm of sustainability calls for consideration of the overall impact of agriculture on the environment. The center's space is comprised of various experiential facilities that reveal the direction of future agricultural development. The program also consists of various experiential activities based on scientific thinking within agriculture.

To realize the value of sustainable agriculture sought by the center, each program organizes youth activities according to specific themes related to agriculture. For example, the "Horizon Harvest Dance (rice farming line dance)" is based on understanding the various stages of farming, including the cultivation environment of rice crops, and enables youth to experience the stages indirectly through dancing. With the exception of ecological content-oriented "Wetland Ecological Life," most programs focus on creating youth experiences using various modes of expression, communication, and the acquisition of scientific knowledge regarding agriculture, food, life sciences, biotechnology, and nature. However, since many students of the school group participate in the program's two-night, three-day youth training activities, the program makes use of existing youth training activities that focus on community activities. Therefore, the program has attempted changes to enable indirect experience of agricultural life factors to allow many students to experience farming at the same time.

On the other hand, the "Secret Garden," which is actively linked with the local community, is a camp-based program for small-scale schools and youth. This program, inspired by the guerrilla gardening of the UK, is designed to teach youth basic skills, such as making resource recycling pots, planting and growing horticultural plants or crops, and helping youth contribute to the beautification of their communities. Thus, this program aims to instill confidence in youth to enable them to play an active role in society. It enlightens their civic consciousness and sense of responsibility through direct participation in the revegetation of local backyard spaces. It also enhances their peer relationships by managing them with their peers. Therefore, we plan to develop this as a UNESCO ESD official project to achieve sustainable cities and agriculture.

Table 4. Case of National Youth Agriculture and Life Center Program in Gimje

Case Program	Content	Target
Horizon Harvest Dance (Group training activity)	Understanding the various processes of rice cultivation by learning the dance movement (line dance) and making and expressing the dance movements related to crop cultivation by themselves to enhance their understanding of agriculture and promote a sense of closeness and interactions among peers.	Less than 250 elementary and middle school students (all times)
Horizon Natural Bingo (Group training activity)	Consists of various missions to reflect youths' perspectives related to natural objects based on the observation of natural ecology using the center's outdoor environment. Activities are carried out by groups, and the photos taken with tablet PCs during the missions are shared on the overhead projector on the last day.	Less than 250 elementary and middle school students (all times)
Wetland Ecological Life (A single specialized program)	Aims to enhance understanding and a sense of closeness with wetland ecosystem and recognize the value of biodiversity through ecological exploration of paddy wetlands. It consists of lectures on wetlands, biological sampling in the surrounding paddy wetlands, and scientific inquiry activities through observation in the laboratory.	Less than 40 middle and high school students (June-October)
Energy Bar Making (Family camp-based operation. Total two hours)	Focuses on raising awareness of the importance of food and future direction of agriculture using rice (the main product of Gimje) and establishing the right standards for food selection through experiencing the cooking process of processed food.	Elementary and middle school students and their families (all times)
Secret Garden (1 night 2 days camp)	Urban participation activities, such as making pots using waste materials and planting vegetation in local devastated areas. It gives significance to youth participation in communities beyond horticulture education, such as making seed bags and distributing them to the elderly, planting plants on untreated roads, and hanging plastic pots on school walls. It focuses on cultivating community spirit through the group activities of participating youth and municipalities and develops creativity through the formation of a green cultural space.	Less than 40 middle and high school students (spring/fall) (affiliated with Gimje City Hall and Gimje Office of Education)

4.2. Exploring the Program Effect on Youth Sustainability Competency

The goals of these programs from the viewpoint of SDGs hold that youth competency may be related to "self-identity", especially among the sub-components of the self-awareness competency. Various activities experienced by the youth emphasize the value of sustainability which will be pursued by agriculture in the future (Horizon Harvest Dance, Energy Bar Making, and Wetland Ecological Life). These activities enable youth to practice the value in their lives (Energy Bar Making) as independent citizens in society (Secret Garden).

Next, in terms of the inquiry competency, the value is emphasized explicitly through activities in which the youth proactively participate, such as Horizon Natural Bingo and Secret Garden. In addition, several programs (such as I Am Now a Plant Doctor) also develop youth competency so they can observe, explore, and express the biodiversity and natural phenomena regularly found in agricultural ecology. The program emphasizes a more integrated viewpoint related to sustainable agriculture (which examines the present situation and presents exploratory projects in which youth can participate) is developed to realize the values of sustainable agriculture and will therefore be able to contribute to the development of critical, reflective, and systems thinking-related competencies.

In the integrated problem-solving competency, empathy, sensitivity, communication, and collaboration are directly reflected in various programs. First, various interpretations of natural objects (Horizon Natural Bingo) and paddy ecological field experience (Wetland Ecological Life) help develop sensitivity regarding nature. Diverse coordination and role-sharing in community activities will contribute to the development of communication skills among peers. The "Secret Garden" program differs from these community programs in that it specifically addresses creative problem-solving factors. The youth plant vegetation in underserved areas or distribute seeds to the elderly. Such activities are directly related to contributing to society as democratic citizens. Moreover, the youth proactively express their opinions on the locations in which seeds are sown, to whom they distribute pots, and in so doing, they reflect on and consider practical feasibility. In this process, they simultaneously experience the successes and limitations of community participation.

With the exception of the "Secret Garden," the remaining programs are operated as part of the accommodation program, so the youth participate in the preplanned program rather than arranging the content and methods of the activities independently. This program revealed differences in the degree of youth participation. For example, in "Energy Bar Making," lectures on agriculture and food are short. The "Energy Bar Making" program consists of a series of experiential processes in which the youth make their own energy bars and package them, thereby generating a positive response from the youth. The youth become naturally interested in the program, as they can gain fresh experiences that they do not otherwise encounter in everyday life, such as handling processed food-making machines and observing the process of labeling the processed year and month during packaging.

In contrast, "Horizon Natural Bingo," which took place outdoors at the center, required significant effort from the instructor to stimulate the interest of the youth; many did not care for outdoor activities. The instructor proposed the use of a tablet PC to record mission activities that required participants to observe natural objects and interpret them from their own perspectives, such as "finding numbers in trees" and "finding natural objects with a similar size to one's head." These missions were conducted in groups, and before the mission, the group members volunteered for one of several roles, such as photographer, bingo strategist, communication arbitrator between the members, and action leader. The highlight of this program was the point at which each group gathered in the auditorium after finishing their activity's objectives and saw photos taken during the activity on a large screen. The youth enjoyed seeing their own faces and those of their friends blended in with various objects in nature and were able to develop an organic understanding of different viewpoints on natural objects.

Nature Bingo makes the youth to do their own, so our intervention may cause problems. Therefore, we are always at the crossroads. I always do not like to intervene, but I contemplate whether I should encourage them. Some students encourage other like a cheerleader. Because they have their own roles, I try to trust them. However, I always consider whether it is right to just look at them. (instructor interview)

The programs have been developed and operated by center instructors for the past four years. The instructors' majors are varied, and focus on topics such as agriculture, life sciences, environmental engineering, and the arts, thereby naturally creating a collaborative atmosphere. For example, the instructor in charge of the "Horizon Natural Bingo" program majored in agriculture. The instructor learned and applied ideas about how to work closely with the youth and assign roles to elicit their active participation from other instructors who majored in youth education, thereby improving the effectiveness of the programs.

When I first heard about this center in the school, I came up with an image of farmers. When I asked my friends about this center, they also thought of farmers working under the sun. However, when I came here, I realized that agricultural life was not just about farming and farmers but rather it involved psychology, environment, seed, rice plants, agricultural technology, and exchange of labor, the areas we are actually applying to our programs. So whenever I develop a program or plan a project, I feel that the scope of my thinking has been expanded (instructor interview).

CONCLUSION

In these case studies, scientific concepts related to food, agriculture, ecology, energy, and plants characterize the learning contexts in which youth develop their sense of self-identity and positioning in the world. This means that the reorientation of science education to address SDGs issues is possible through community-based, interdisciplinary, and youth-centered programs. However, much work still needs to be done to elucidate the concepts and components of the youth sustainability competency.

Furthermore, other areas of SDGs such as poverty, wellbeing of community members, and sustainable lifestyles have not been thoroughly addressed within the traditional science education context and need to be explored in ways which incorporate science and technology to address those issues.

REFERENCES

de Haan, G. (2006). "The BLK '21' programme in Germany: a 'Gestaltungskompetenz'-based model for education for sustainable development", *Environmental Education Research*, *12*(1), 19-32.

Elsevier. (2015). *Sustainability Science in a Global Landscape*. Elsevier.

Feinstein, N. W. & Kircgasler, K. L. (2015). Sustainability in Science Education? How the Next Generation Science Standards Approach Sustainability, and Why It Matters. *Science Education*, *99*(1), 121-144.

Hackmann, H. (2017). Editorial. *Environmental Scientist*, September 2017.

Hwang, S., Lee, Y. & Cho, S. (2017). *Developing Youth Environmental Education Activities for Promoting Youth Competencies in the SDGs era*. National Youth Policy Institute: Sejong, Republic of Korea.

Lotz-Sisitka, H. & Raven, G. (2009). South Africa: applied competence as the guiding framework for environmental and sustainability education. In Fien, J., Maclean, R. & Park, M. G. (Eds). Work, Learning and Sustainable Development: Opportunities and Challenges. *UNEVOC Technical and Vocational Education & Training Series*, *8*, 308-318. Heidelberg: Springer.

Mogensen, F. & Schnack, K. (2010). The action competence approach and the 'new' discourses of education for sustainable development, competence and quality criteria. *Environmental Education Research*, *16*(1), 59-74.

UNESCO. (2017). *Education for Sustainable Development Goals: Learning Objectives*. Paris: UNESCO.

INDEX

A

academic learning, 24
academic success, 5
accounting, 101, 113, 115, 117
acquisition of knowledge, 138
action research, 45
activity status report on the education system and systematic steps for its development, 74, 75, 76, 77, 94
adolescents, x, 99, 100, 120, 121, 123
adult learning, 54, 56
adulthood, 54, 124
adults, 25, 26, 27, 134
agency(ies), vii, viii, 1, 2, 4, 5, 10, 12, 13, 14, 16, 17, 19, 20, 21, 22, 35, 36, 39, 43, 44, 46, 48, 123, 124, 130, 134
agriculture, 139, 140, 141, 142, 143, 144
American Educational Research Association, 94
American Psychological Association, 123
architect, 105, 112, 113
assessment, 61, 84, 86, 124
atmosphere, 109, 110, 144
attitudes, 23, 48, 65, 66, 69, 73, 75, 79, 80, 86

automation, 75, 106, 108, 110, 111
autonomy, 7, 52, 77, 119
awareness, 23, 39, 46, 68, 130, 131, 132, 134, 135, 136, 137, 138, 139, 141, 142

B

basic education, 70, 72, 79, 96
basic school, vii, ix, 63, 64, 67, 68, 69, 70, 71, 73, 76, 77, 78, 79, 80, 82, 86, 88, 89, 91, 96
behaviors, 102, 129, 130
biodiversity, vii, x, 125, 141, 142
biological sciences, 41
biotechnology, 140

C

case study(ies), 39, 56, 103, 126, 144
challenges, vii, x, 41, 64, 121, 125, 127
childhood, 29, 107, 109, 110, 112, 114, 121
children, 6, 7, 16, 18, 25, 27, 41, 52, 61, 67, 68, 91, 109
citizens, 8, 27, 37, 92, 130, 142
classes, 43, 77, 87, 111, 115, 119

148 *Index*

classroom, viii, x, 8, 9, 10, 11, 16, 17, 49, 50, 52, 55, 59, 61, 125
classroom environment, 11
climate, vii, x, 10, 125, 127, 128, 129, 139
climate change, vii, x, 125, 127, 128, 129, 139
collaboration, 132, 138, 142
college students, 32, 46, 124
communication, 7, 48, 55, 66, 84, 135, 136, 142, 143
communication technologies, 66
communities, 10, 14, 15, 18, 45, 46, 60, 130, 133, 134, 137, 140, 141
community, viii, x, 16, 26, 39, 41, 42, 43, 46, 50, 53, 54, 69, 125, 126, 127, 131, 132, 133, 134, 135, 137, 138, 140, 141, 142, 144
competences in science and technology, 68, 69
compulsory education, 45, 66
computer, 83, 100, 107, 108, 113
conditions for technology teaching, 85, 86
conference, 53, 58, 65, 93, 123, 139
construction, viii, 1, 4, 29, 32, 46, 48, 77, 110, 119
cooperation, 126, 129, 130
creative teaching, 56
creative thinking, 72
creativity, 73, 122, 141
critical thinking, 130, 133, 137
criticism, 21, 71, 75, 89
cultivation, 137, 140, 141
cultural conditions, 32
cultural heritage, 72
cultural stereotypes, 102, 118
culture, ix, 18, 20, 23, 25, 32, 48, 49, 63, 64, 65, 69, 135, 138
curricula, ix, 53, 64, 68, 77, 83, 84, 95
curriculum, 8, 49, 56, 65, 66, 70, 71, 76, 77, 79, 80, 81, 82, 84, 85, 86, 87, 88, 118, 124

curriculum reform, 70, 71, 76, 77, 79, 80, 81, 84, 86, 88

D

demographic characteristics, 102
Department of Education, 57, 59
didactic teaching, 77
discrimination, 23, 88
disposition, 3, 6, 8, 54
diversity, 9, 10, 16, 18, 126, 129, 132

E

ecology, 141, 142, 144
economic status, 3, 21
ecosystem, 127, 129, 141
education, vii, ix, x, 2, 4, 5, 6, 8, 11, 13, 19, 21, 26, 36, 37, 40, 41, 42, 45, 46, 47, 48, 49, 50, 53, 55, 56, 57, 59, 60, 63, 64, 65, 66, 67, 68, 69, 70, 71, 72, 74, 75, 76, 77, 78, 79, 80, 81, 82, 83, 86, 88, 90, 92, 93, 94, 95, 96, 97, 99, 100, 103, 105, 106,107, 108, 111, 112, 114, 115, 118, 123, 125, 127, 128, 129, 130, 132, 139, 141, 144, 145
education policy, ix, 64, 78
educational institutions, 90
educational research, 2, 58
educators, 8, 10, 17, 18, 37, 40, 51
e-learning, 61
empathy, 129, 131, 142
employers, 5, 76, 77, 91, 92
employment, 5, 8, 13, 65, 68, 73, 104
employment status, 104
empowerment, 60, 127
encouragement, 106, 107, 113, 114, 116, 117
energy, vii, x, 10, 24, 29, 121, 125, 127, 143, 144

Index

engineering, x, 40, 50, 53, 56, 66, 99, 100, 107, 110, 115, 117, 119, 120, 121, 122, 123, 124, 144
environmental change, 132
environmental issues, 127
environmental technology, 114
environment(s), 11, 52, 68, 69, 73, 76, 108, 110, 113, 132, 133, 135, 138, 139, 140, 141, 144
equality, 10, 100, 127
equipment, 72, 75, 77, 83, 85, 88, 89
ethnicity, viii, 2, 5, 6, 10, 13, 14, 16, 19, 21, 35, 40, 50
European Parliament, 68, 69, 93
European Union, ix, 64, 66, 78, 93
everyday life, 73, 113, 143

F

families, 5, 6, 13, 14, 141
feelings, 23, 43, 59, 87, 88, 131
fluid, viii, 2, 3, 23, 25, 27, 28, 36, 37, 38, 39, 41, 43, 45
food, 106, 133, 134, 135, 137, 138, 139, 140, 141, 143, 144
force, viii, 2, 25, 43, 46, 71, 92, 134
foreign language, 86, 89
formation, 3, 12, 22, 25, 35, 48, 79, 134, 141
funding, 13, 46, 83, 91

G

gender differences, 56, 117
gender equality, 100, 127
gender inequality, 7
gender role, 102, 118
general education, ix, 63, 65, 67, 86
global forces, viii, 2, 4, 5, 11, 12, 13, 14, 15, 17, 18, 25, 41, 44
global warming, 121, 127

governments, ix, 13, 64
grades, 49, 67, 71, 82, 85, 86, 88, 107, 108, 110, 112, 113, 115, 119
greenhouse gas emissions, 128
growth, 3, 49, 61, 92, 127

H

health, 13, 41, 61, 73, 127, 129, 132, 137, 138
health condition, 13, 41
high school, 7, 15, 49, 50, 51, 100, 106, 113, 115, 119, 123, 124, 141
higher education, 53, 55, 59, 91
human activity, 72, 73, 103

I

identity, v, vii, viii, 1, 2, 3, 4, 5, 8, 9, 10, 11, 12, 13, 14, 15, 16, 18, 19, 20, 21, 22, 23, 24, 25, 26, 27, 28, 29, 30, 31, 32, 33, 34, 35, 36, 37, 38, 39, 40, 41, 42, 43, 44, 45, 46, 47, 48, 49, 50, 51, 52, 53, 54, 55, 57, 58, 132, 134, 135, 137, 142, 144
image, 136, 144
individual characteristics, 102, 118
individuality, 13, 17, 18, 20, 25
individuals, viii, 2, 5, 9, 11, 12, 18, 22, 23, 25, 27, 35, 37, 41, 45, 52, 57, 68, 75, 102, 117, 120
inequality, 7, 122, 127
inequity, 100, 101
information technology, 83, 86, 105
institutions, 12, 13, 14, 75, 90
intentionality, 4, 25, 28, 30
internship, x, 125, 133, 134, 135, 136, 137, 138
intervention, 27, 45, 144
intervention strategies, 45

Index

L

labor market, ix, 64, 72, 77, 78, 89, 90, 92
languages, 86, 111
leadership, 86, 127, 131, 132, 134
learners, viii, 1, 2, 3, 18, 24, 26
learning, vii, viii, x, 1, 2, 3, 9, 10, 15, 17, 18, 22, 23, 24, 25, 26, 34, 38, 39, 44, 45, 46, 49, 50, 51, 52, 53, 54, 56, 58, 59, 60, 61, 125, 128, 129, 133, 134, 137, 141, 144
learning process, 25, 59
Learning Slovakia, 75, 76, 78, 95
legislation, ix, 64, 78, 93
lens, vii, viii, 1, 2, 24, 47, 49, 50
level of education, 70
life changes, 25
life experiences, 24, 25
life sciences, 140, 144
lifelong learning, 25, 45, 46
light, viii, 1, 10, 46, 111, 134
literacy, 8, 9, 21, 56, 68, 82, 123
local community, 41, 42, 131, 134, 135, 140
lower secondary education, vii, ix, 63, 67, 70, 76, 96

M

manual skills, 67, 73, 85
materials, 72, 73, 77, 82, 83, 84, 85, 87, 88, 113, 121, 134, 141
mathematics, 7, 9, 40, 49, 51, 53, 56, 66, 107, 109, 112, 115, 116
mathematics education, 49, 56
measurement, vii, x, 99, 118, 120
medical, 41, 42, 115, 121
medical science, 41, 42, 115, 121
meta-analysis, 123, 124
methodology, 78, 103
middle class, 3, 6, 43
middle-class families, 6

migration, 37, 38, 39, 49
military, 13, 108, 110
mission(s), 73, 79, 90, 141, 143
models, vii, viii, 1, 2, 5, 28, 44
models of identity, 11, 28
modernization, ix, 64, 78, 88
mortality rate, 27
motivated behavioral choice(s), v, x, 99, 100, 101, 102, 103, 104, 107, 108, 109, 110, 111, 112, 113, 115, 116, 117, 120, 121
motivation, 7, 49, 101, 109, 119, 122, 129

N

national development program of education and training, 75, 95
natural science, 93, 106
neglect, 16, 45
networking, 29, 120

O

OECD, 66, 95
opportunities, 16, 21, 41, 42, 46, 73, 83, 88, 89, 116, 127, 137
organize, 72, 73, 114
outreach, 18, 19, 26
outreach programs, 26

P

parental involvement, 5, 124
parental support, 51
parenting styles, 7
parents, viii, 2, 3, 5, 6, 7, 16, 27, 35, 40, 43, 47, 70, 77, 84, 90, 91, 92, 105, 116, 119, 120, 123
Parliament, 68, 69, 93

Index

151

participants, 14, 15, 101, 104, 106, 117, 118, 119, 121, 138, 143

peer relationship, 119, 138, 140

personal efficacy, 118

personal identity, 2, 4, 5, 32, 132

personal interview, ix, 64, 78, 80, 81, 82

personality, 25, 28, 29, 30, 31, 36, 49, 123, 138

physical sciences, 115, 121

physics, 10, 17, 25, 40, 50, 51, 53, 58, 60, 66, 82, 85, 87, 100, 107, 109

plants, 140, 141, 144

policy, ix, 64, 78, 127

population, viii, 1, 8, 119

poverty, 20, 127, 145

primary education, 65, 67, 106

primary school, 39, 48, 94, 105, 110

principles, 68, 69, 72, 126, 131

problem-solving, 8, 130, 131, 132, 133, 138, 142

professional careers, 122

professionals, 8, 41, 44, 136

project, 45, 47, 58, 129, 133, 140, 144

prosperity, 64, 126, 127

psychology, 53, 144

Q

qualifications, 6, 21, 46

qualitative research, 60

quality of life, 127

R

race, viii, 2, 5, 6, 13, 14, 35, 40, 50

reality, vii, ix, 63, 64, 66, 69, 78, 89, 126

reasoning, 69, 119

recognition, 14, 16, 17, 19

recommendation of the European Parliament and the council on key competences for lifelong learning, 68

reform(s), vii, ix, 64, 65, 66, 68, 70, 71, 76, 77, 78, 79, 80, 81, 84, 86, 87, 88, 97

regression, 42, 43, 44

reinforcement, 66, 69

rejection, 31, 89

relevance, 56, 90, 118

religion, 3, 5, 35, 40

requirement(s), 10, 68, 70, 75, 76, 77, 80, 85, 87, 91, 92

researchers, 40, 45

resilience, 132, 136

resources, 4, 11, 14, 19, 27, 30, 42, 48, 77, 83, 85, 89, 127, 137

response, 12, 20, 54, 68, 128, 143

reviews of the nature of identity, 4

rules, 4, 72, 95

S

safety, 69, 72, 74, 132, 134

scholarship, 59, 61, 107

school education program, 70, 71, 77, 82

school facilities, 83, 88

science identity, vii, viii, 1, 2, 3, 5, 8, 9, 10, 11, 13, 14, 15, 17, 18, 19, 35, 37, 38, 39, 40, 44, 48, 49, 55, 57, 58

scientific knowledge, 21, 46, 128, 140

scope, 65, 75, 128, 144

secondary education, vii, ix, 63, 64, 65, 67, 70, 76, 78, 79, 96

secondary school students, 57, 96

secondary schools, 66, 70, 91, 92, 105, 113

secondary students, 50

secondary vocational schools, 75, 76, 92

security, 4, 16, 73

segregation, vii, x, 40, 99, 100

self-awareness, 130, 132, 135, 142

self-confidence, 17, 102, 106, 113, 114, 116, 117, 120, 121

self-efficacy, 18, 19, 122, 132

self-identity, 27, 34, 50, 132, 134, 135, 142, 144

self-perceptions, 15, 24, 29, 33, 36

self-reflection, 24, 134

self-reports, 103, 107, 121

sex differences, 119, 123, 124

Slovakia, v, vii, ix, 63, 64, 67, 68, 69, 74, 75, 76, 77, 78, 79, 80, 92, 93, 94, 95, 96

social agents, 5, 10, 11, 12, 13, 14, 15, 17, 18, 44

social class, 3, 5, 21, 77

social context, 6, 12, 22, 102

social development, 69, 126

social influence, 32, 49, 58

social interaction, vii, viii, 1, 10, 29

social network, 21, 120

social structure, vii, viii, 1, 4, 11, 21

society, ix, 5, 18, 20, 48, 50, 52, 63, 64, 66, 68, 72, 75, 93, 94, 126, 128, 129, 130, 131, 140, 142

sociology, 48, 49

solidarity, 49, 129

solution, 71, 81, 131

stability, viii, 2, 5, 11, 12, 15, 27, 30, 37, 39, 40, 43, 45, 134

stable identity, 2

state education program, 70, 71, 82, 84, 85, 86, 89, 90, 96

stereotypes, 102, 118

structure, 2, 4, 5, 19, 21, 28, 29, 30, 31, 48, 67, 70, 92, 123, 124

structure of the school system, 92

student development, 46, 52

subject matter content, 83

survey research, ix, 63, 64, 79, 80, 88

sustainability, vii, x, 69, 125, 126, 129, 130, 131, 132, 133, 134, 139, 142, 144, 145

sustainable development goals (SDGs), v, vii, x, 125, 126, 127, 128, 130, 131, 132, 133, 139, 142, 144, 145

T

talent, 100, 105, 106, 111, 112, 113, 114, 116, 117, 118, 121

teacher training, 77, 84, 88

teachers, viii, ix, 2, 3, 5, 6, 9, 10, 11, 12, 13, 16, 17, 18, 27, 35, 40, 41, 43, 45, 51, 56, 57, 63, 64, 68, 77, 78, 80, 81, 82, 83, 84, 85, 86, 87, 88, 89, 91, 104, 108, 116, 119, 120, 124, 135

teaching technology, ix, 64, 81, 83, 86, 87

technical study branches, 66

techniques, 65, 72, 75

technological competence, vii, x, 99, 100, 103, 104, 107, 109, 110, 111, 114, 116, 118, 119, 120

technological progress, 69

technological talent(s), 100, 101, 106, 111, 112, 114, 117, 118, 121, 122

technologically talented, x, 100, 101, 104, 117, 119, 120

technologies, 59, 65, 66, 72, 75, 128

technology, v, vii, ix, x, 47, 53, 54, 55, 56, 60, 63, 64, 65, 66, 67, 68, 69, 70, 71, 72, 73, 74, 76, 78, 79, 80, 81, 82, 83, 84, 85, 86, 87, 88, 89, 90, 91, 92, 93, 94, 95, 96, 99, 100, 101, 103, 104, 105, 106, 107, 108, 109, 110, 111, 112, 113, 114, 115, 117, 118, 119, 120, 121, 122, 123, 124, 125, 126, 144, 145

technology education, vii, ix, xi, 47, 63, 64, 65, 66, 67, 68, 69, 70, 71, 76, 78, 81, 88, 95, 96, 100, 103, 105, 107, 108, 111, 112, 114, 115, 118, 123, 126

technology teachers, ix, 64, 78, 80, 87, 89, 91

technology-based society, 66, 93

training, 11, 67, 70, 71, 75, 76, 77, 84, 88, 93, 105, 106, 113, 115, 119, 140, 141

transformational learning, viii, 1, 2, 3, 22, 24, 34, 38

Index

153

transformation(s), viii, 1, 15, 20, 22, 23, 25, 26, 27, 28, 29, 36, 37, 39, 40, 41, 42, 43, 44, 45, 53, 54, 57, 136
transition to adulthood, 124
triggers, viii, 2, 10, 24, 26, 27, 32, 35, 38, 39, 54

U

UNESCO, 65, 96, 124, 128, 130, 131, 140, 145
United Nations Development Program (UNDP), 127
universities, viii, 1, 45, 59, 61, 129
urban, 15, 48, 49, 52, 133, 134

V

vision(s), vii, x, 74, 83, 84, 91, 125, 127, 130, 131
vocational education, ix, 64, 75, 76, 78
vocational education and training, 75, 76
vocational training, 75, 77

W

Warsaw Pact, 67
web, 95, 96, 102
work activities, 73
work education, 67, 68, 70
workers, 5, 13, 37, 67
workforce, 75, 100
working class, 3, 41
working conditions, 72
workload, 87
workplace, 53, 100
workrooms, 73, 83, 84, 86, 88

Y

young adults, 27
young people, x, 3, 5, 6, 11, 21, 45, 58, 66, 68, 120, 125
youth, v, x, 5, 13, 37, 49, 60, 64, 68, 76, 93, 101, 124, 125, 126, 127, 128, 129, 130, 132, 133, 134, 135, 136, 137, 138, 139, 140, 141, 142, 143, 144, 145
youth sustainability competency, x, 125, 126, 130, 132, 134, 144